CW00706915

How to Eat An Elephant

How to tackle any challenge ... and succeed

Dedication

To Mindy who helped me through the birth pangs and Neil whose unfailing support helped me through the tough times, and all my friends who helped with the final finishing touches.

How to

EAT AN ELEPHANT

How to tackle any challenge ... and succeed

Jo Parker

How To Eat An Elephant

How to tackle any challenge ... and succeed

First published in 2011 by
Ecademy Press
48 St Vincent Drive, St Albans, Herts, AL1 5SJ
info@ecademy-press.com
www.ecademy-press.com

Printed and Bound by Lightning Source in the UK and USA
Artwork by Karen Gladwell
Cover design by Michael Inns

Printed on acid-free paper from managed forests. This book is
printed on demand, so no copies will be remaindered or pulped.

ISBN 978-1-907722-00-4

Contents

CHAPTER ONE

Why bother?

Do some challenges seem daunting?

Have you ever read in newspapers or magazines about people who tackled huge tasks, like launching a new business or organising a grand event, and thought to yourself 'I'd love to try something like that but I just wouldn't know where to start'? Or perhaps there's something you'd like to do but it just seems too big a task – changing job, moving house, organising a big charity event. Some challenges may put you off because something will take such a long time. How will you keep going, maintain momentum, keep track of what you need to do?

Something quite straightforward, such as having a good clear-out, can seem like a huge and challenging task on top of everything else. Even quite small tasks can leave you wondering how on earth you'll manage to get everything done and often you can feel like a juggler, desperately trying to keep all the balls in the air and wondering what will happen if you drop one.

You are not alone

Shall I let you into a secret? You are not alone. There are lots of people who would love to have a go at something but don't give it a try because they feel overwhelmed by the task or just don't know where to start.

In order to raise money for charity, I do lot of speaking at Women's Institutes. I talk about my wedding which was held on the edge of Antarctica on the island of South Georgia, the year I worked in Afghanistan and how I compete in triathlons. After the talks I get all sorts of women who come up to me and say 'I'd love to have a go at a triathlon but I just wouldn't know where to start' or 'I'd love to work abroad but I just don't know how to go about it'. Some of them even tell me about the wedding they have volunteered to organise for their daughter and how they half-wish the selfsame daughter would go off to Antarctica to get married like I did so they wouldn't have the huge challenge of organising their wedding.

If you talk to these people, it turns out that they do organise all sorts of other things – Women's Institute meetings, village events, outings for friends and family. However, trying something rather different worries them and they just don't know what to do.

Others don't even own up to it. At most, they talk about their 'friend' who doesn't know what to do, but with such a close knowledge that I can't help speculating whether that friend is actually them. That leaves me wondering if there are others out there who don't even own up to having a daydream. They keep it close in their heart but never realise it as they feel the challenge is too big.

Not everyone admits to their dreams

There are all sorts of reasons why people don't own up to having a dream. Some feel they have no right to want something as grand or as ambitious. Sadly, in the UK many people still feel they should not have 'ideas above their station'. Often they are afraid that people will ridicule their ambitions. I remember when I had my annual appraisal with one boss; he asked what my ambition was. I replied honestly that I'd love to be a director of a company. He laughed at me and told me that was rather ambitious. That was in 1992. In 2000 I was made director of North Surrey Water Company.

Admittedly, I was director for less than a year as it was decided at my first board meeting to merge with my old company. Still, it gave me huge satisfaction to know that I'd proved the sceptical boss from my past wrong (although he had retired by that time).

Some people don't own up to an ambition because they are worried that their colleagues or friends may try to put them off it. Someone wanting to lose weight may be told 'but you're nice the way you are'. Someone wanting to change jobs may well not tell their colleagues at work – and certainly not their boss! Someone thinking of taking up a new hobby might be asked 'Why do you want to do that?'

There can be pressure from family and friends to stay as you are. They may not want to venture into unfamiliar territory even if you are up for it. Some people may have spent so much of their life putting family first that actually tackling something for themselves may feel wrong. However, doing anything differently will feel strange at first; it's only after a while that it becomes habitual. Try this little exercise: clasp your hands in front of you; notice whether your right or your left little finger is at the back; now change your fingers over so that the other little finger is at the back. Does that feel strange? Leave it for a while and it will start to feel 'normal'. Any change can be like that and feels strange when you first do it, but if you keep on doing it for long enough it will become normal for you.

Sometimes people don't own up to a grand plan because they are worried that, by voicing what they want, they will be expected to do something about it. They might quite like the humdrum rut they are trundling along and, although they have daydreams, realising those dreams could actually be quite frightening. It would take them away from the familiar and safe existence they have now.

I can understand that fear as I suffered from it myself. When I was younger, I had the opportunity to be sponsored by a local rotary club to study overseas for a year. Although I was short-listed for the award, I later pulled out as I had a nice flat and was worried that I might not find another place as nice to live in when I returned. When it was too late, I was really sorry I'd thrown away such an opportunity. I also decided against applying for some jobs as I wasn't sure what they would bring and wasn't even sure I could do the job. It wasn't until I started admitting these things to my friends that I found out that quite a few of them had done similar things.

Why a comfortable rut is not such a good thing

One could ask 'Why shouldn't I stay in a rut if it's comfortable?' The problem is that nothing in this world stays still; everything is growing or diminishing. Even the most solid-looking stones are being eroded slowly and seemingly still water will be flowing or evaporating. The same applies to us. We may think we are standing still, but if we don't stretch ourselves, then in fact we tend to gradually retreat into a smaller and smaller comfort zone. Maybe there's something we used to do but we haven't done it for weeks, then months and then years. Before you know it, it's been such a long time that it becomes too much effort.

I'm sure lots of people have found this with friends. If you don't get in touch with them, it can become more and more difficult to contact them until sometimes you just lose touch and never see them again. That might not be a problem, but if you don't make new friends your circle of friends may gradually get smaller and smaller.

Cope with the unexpected challenges

In the same way, our ability to tackle new challenges may decrease if we don't keep exercising that ability. When we are young everything is novel but, as we get older, we have fewer and fewer new experiences. That can mean that when you have no choice about tackling something new it can be really tough. Even if you think that doesn't matter, you can't assume that life will stay the same. Life doesn't always go the way you expect. Divorce, bereavement and redundancy can hit unexpectedly and the more one is used to dealing with new circumstances and taking on new challenges, the easier it is to cope when something comes along you hadn't foreseen.

A friend of mine is great at tackling projects. She's gained all sorts of qualifications through studying part-time which has helped her grow her business. It also made her a stronger person and, when her husband was offered a job in the Middle East, although it was a daunting task to pack up the house and move herself and her two teenage sons to join him, her strength kept her going through the toughest challenge she'd ever had to meet.

Taking on a challenge

As I mentioned, I had always tended to stay with what I knew. However, I grew increasingly frustrated when a certain job I wanted kept eluding me. I kept being told I didn't have the experience, but that left me in a Catch 22 situation as I needed the job to get the experience. Eventually, I had an opportunity to gain the experience but it would have meant working overseas for a year – and not just anywhere but in Afghanistan during the height of the civil war there. It was a tough decision and I had no idea how I would get on. However, this time I decided I wouldn't take the 'safe' route and I said yes to the opportunity. I had a wonderful time in Afghanistan. Even though there were times when I found it really tough, I weathered the storms and as I did so I gained more strength and understanding about myself. I felt like a completely different person when I returned. Back in the UK I got the long sought-after job and took on fresh challenges. I found that as I did so I grew stronger and stronger.

One of my toughest challenges came when my company restructured. I had the choice of transferring to a job in Folkestone or redundancy. As I had just met a wonderful man who lived in Bedfordshire, Folkestone would have made maintaining that relationship difficult. I therefore accepted the redundancy offer and decided to start my own business after 28 years as an employee. That was one of the most difficult things I had ever tackled, particularly as I then decided to move house as well. However, my earlier challenges stood me in good stead and when I had moved house and set up my new office and was finding that work was coming in steadily, I also realised that again I had reached an even higher level of confidence.

Challenges can get easier

It's surprising how something which can seem too daunting can, over time and with repetition, get easier and easier. Before you know it, what seemed an impossible hill to climb is behind you and you're relishing the next ascent. Besides equipping you to cope with life's knocks, you can acquire new skills which may help with your work, introduce you to new friends or even start a lifetime interest. I found this when writing this book. It was tough at first; I wanted to say so much but didn't know where to start and never found the time. With some help, I managed to order my thoughts and, once I started, it got easier and easier to write.

Create the life you want

Another benefit of taking on the big challenges is that you are able to create for yourself the life you want. I've already explained how taking the job overseas gave me the experience I needed for the job I wanted back in the UK. I had started to turn my life into what I really wanted it to be.

I also decided to study for a further qualification through distance learning. That was another huge challenge, but I came to find the new subjects fascinating and I found exercising my brain really rewarding. Initially, finding the time and the discipline was really difficult but gradually I got into a routine and I found it easier and easier. The course equipped me for some new jobs and helped me gain promotion.

Couch potato to triathlete

One thing I'd always wanted was to feel fitter and to be slimmer. I'd always been hopeless at games – the sort of person who didn't make it into the form team and ended up pushing a ball around at the back of the hockey nets or throwing it against the wall of the gym. A few years ago, a friend suggested that I have a go at a triathlon. This required swimming 400m – I could barely swim a length. I had to cycle 25km – probably the easiest of the three tasks. Finally I had to run 5km. Running was something I found really tough; I had tried jogging a few times, but found it hard to keep going. However, with help and encouragement from my friend, I had a go. Competing in that first triathlon has transformed my life. I am now fitter and slimmer than I've ever been in my life. At long last I can choose clothes that I like, rather than because they fit. I have more energy and don't get ill. Finally I really have created the life I wanted. In the same way, you can transform your life in lots of ways. You do not have to stick with the same job in the same location with the same activities when you get back home.

You will see in this book that I use the example of competing in my first triathlon quite a few times. It was something I didn't feel capable of initially but which really did transform my life. However, to finish my first triathlon required me to use all my skills as a project manager – only this time I was the project!

Never stop learning

Even now, taking on new 'big tasks' stretches and toughens me. Recently I was asked to act as an expert witness in a major planning enquiry. This was something I had never done before. I had to analyse the performance of another company and write a report which would be considered in detail by the other side's legal experts. I would have to justify all my statements and explain why I had made them. I would even be cross-examined by a senior member of the legal profession – and all this in front of former colleagues as well as the national press. It was without doubt the toughest thing I'd had to cope with yet. I had three days of questioning by a top London lawyer, during which time I was not allowed to speak to any of the team I had worked with. However, when it was finished I really did feel I could tackle anything. The confidence boost has helped me as a person and helped my business.

It is possible to change

I hope that from my examples you can see that it is possible to change the way you feel about life or even about yourself. Lots of people go through life feeling scared, unworthy, inadequate or stuck in a rut. A life coach I knew said that one of the most common problems she came up against was 'the impostor syndrome', where people feel they don't really know enough and are waiting for people to find them out. The truth is that, did they but realise it, a large number of the people around them feel just the same. We put on a veneer of confidence and in some cases, even if we don't know exactly what to do, we muddle through. It's amazing how successful 'muddling through' can be. Of course, knowing a few tricks about how to order one's thoughts and organise one's actions can help ensure that you spot problems and sort them out before they turn into a major disaster. That's what this book is all about.

Each time I tackled one of the challenges I've already described – the triathlon, the work overseas, starting my own business – I was very far from being an expert. I did make mistakes, but weathered them and managed to find ways round the problems. As a result, I learnt and developed as a person.

Don't wait to feel ready

Once you start to realise that you don't need to be a world expert on wedding arrangements, marathon running or getting Auntie Nell resettled in her sheltered accommodation, things do start becoming a lot easier and you will start to feel differently. One of the best and easiest ways to do this is to get stuck in and start tackling those jobs which seem so daunting. If you wait for the day when you feel ready for the challenge, then you'll probably wait your life away.

We all have inner resources

Everyone has far more capability than they realise. When I accepted the post in Afghanistan I was a 'townie' who hated camping and the outdoor life. I never thought I'd be able to march up mountains for hours on end, sleep on the floor in rough mud buildings and survive without any running water or electricity. However, I had a wonderful time. We can all find inner resources and they will come out when needed.

Feel differently about yourself

How we feel about ourselves and perceive ourselves is not written in tablets of stone and we can reinvent ourselves if we choose. There's a saying 'If you keep on doing what you've always done, you'll keep on getting what you've always got'. Changing as a person if you keep on doing the same things, day in day out, may not be easy. However, if you start doing something different, and what better way to do that than to work on getting something you really want, then you can start feeling differently about yourself.

I had always seen myself as a city-based career woman, an engineering manager who liked working with a team of other people. When I met the man who is now my husband, keeping that image was going to be difficult to combine with a relationship with him, as he lived out in the country some way away from my place of work. I moved house, started my own business and now I sport my green wellies and Barbour jacket with pride. I even started a small livestock herd and can talk with confidence about the care and breeding of alpacas. I go to country shows and even help as a marshal at these shows. My life could not be more different from the one I had only a few years ago.

Changing wasn't always straightforward but I wouldn't go back to my old life now if I was paid to. Changing from my old habits has also given me a new view on life and new skills which I can use in my work and at home. My new life is wonderful – living in the country allows me to see all sorts of natural beauty I didn't see when I was a town dweller. I've made new friends, but thanks to email and mobile phones I can still keep in touch with my old friends.

Tackling major projects can bring you what you want

I have also tackled major refurbishment schemes with the houses I owned, which has helped me to get larger houses in better parts of the country. In my very first house, I discovered the bay window, front and roof were completely rotten. I had just spent all my money buying this house and I did not have enough to pay a builder to do the work. I set about rebuilding the front of my house, although I had never done anything on this scale before in my life. I remember the day I started that work so well. As I started to remove the rotten timber, I wondered how long it would take me and whether I could manage all of the work. I had to spend all of my spare time on the project and it took the whole summer. I asked friends at work for advice and picked the brains of people I met at the builder's merchants. It was daunting but I ended up with a house that was not only free from rot, but looked a lot better as well. I then sold the house for quite a lot more than I paid for it as it now looked much better, and I was able to move to a much nicer house in a part of town I loved. Again, attempting a major scheme myself helped me to achieve what I wanted in life.

As you tackle challenges, you'll find the knowledge gained will have all sorts of other benefits. You'll learn new skills which can be put to use for other tasks or will help you up the career ladder. You'll become more organised so that even everyday tasks will become easier. Peter Cohen, a life coach and TV presenter says "Research shows that when we make concrete plans and focus on something we want, not only do we feel more organised and less stressed, we are also more likely to get what we want."

Just do it

With so many good reasons to take on the major tasks, there's really no reason to prevaricate. This book will give you the tools you need to tackle all those big tasks. These techniques aren't gimmicks – they're used to deliver all sorts of major projects. You can deliver big projects too.

Key Points

▼ *Lots of people never realise their dreams*

▼ *This is often due to fear, inertia or just not knowing where to start*

▼ *Tackling new challenges brings lots of benefits*
   it will make you stronger physically and mentally
   it will give you more confidence
   it can transform your life
   it can allow you to have what you want in life
   it will make you feel better about yourself

▼ *You are far stronger mentally and physically than you realise*

▼ *The stronger you are, the better you'll cope with unplanned challenges*

CHAPTER TWO

Anyone can do it

You can tackle any task

In the first chapter I explained why tackling something which you may have thought was beyond you can have huge benefits. The good news is that any major task can be conquered if you remember a few simple rules. This book explains those rules. There's no jargon but there are plenty of pictures – word pictures and real pictures as well as examples from real life.

Tried and tested

These rules are tried and tested and are used by people who make a living from delivering huge projects. They may well have to undertake tasks they have not done before, but the approaches I describe in this book help them achieve the goal. I have collected the rules during a lifetime of tackling a huge variety of challenges – at work, at home and in my social life. Some of the rules I learnt through studying – I was lucky enough to study some aspects with an expert from the European Space Agency as part of my management degree. Others I learnt as part of further training at work, in preparation for managing major business and construction projects. Others I learnt along the way – either from my own mistakes, or because people with more knowledge and experience than me were kind enough to pass that on. Everything is tried and tested and is used in all walks of life.

14

Transferable skills

What I have tried to do with this book is capture all those lessons and explain them in simple language. Some personal development and training uses jargon and appears to be very complicated. Project Management techniques are not exempt from this. However, in this book I have avoided the jargon and made sure that everything is explained simply. I've used examples from my own life where I've taken on challenges. Most of these are from my personal life as many of the situations may be ones you could meet as well. I took the lessons that I'd learnt at work and applied them in a huge variety of situations, from organising parties to competing in sport. I even applied the rules to organising my own wedding!

Planning pays off

I hope this book will help you apply the same rules with the same success. I would suggest that you don't rush into what you have to do. In saying this, I'm very aware that I'm one of the worst culprits for rushing into things. My husband still repeats to me the little saying 'Fail to plan, plan to fail' from time to time and it's true that spending time planning and thinking about things really does work. One of my most successful projects was managing the merger of two companies and, although I'd never done anything like it before, I followed all of the rules in this book to the letter. It seemed a huge challenge, but I put a lot of effort into planning the project and the planning paid off. The merger was very successful and the combined company is still operating.

Eating the elephant

So why is this book called 'How to Eat an Elephant'? Well, trying to eat an elephant might seem like an impossible task. It's far too big to tackle and you might wonder where on earth you should start. How on earth would you cook it, let alone eat it? If you were faced with an elephant as the only thing to eat, there's only one way you could go about it. You'd have to break the elephant up into bite-size chunks, or pieces that are at least manageable and which you can fit in a cooking pot. In the same way, every big job can be broken down into a series of smaller tasks which are more manageable. If you keep going, bite by bite, chunk by chunk, meal by meal, you will finish the elephant in the end. How long it would take would depend on the circumstances: the size of the elephant, what you have to cut it up with and cook it in and how many other people are helping – cutting up the elephant, tending the cooking and, of course, joining in the eating. Similarly, a large job can be done in a number of ways and the time taken may vary according to how many other people are helping.

Bite size chunks

This book will show you how to divide a job into those 'bite-size chunks' and any job can be tackled like this. The job may have a long timescale, possibly stretching over several years. Studying for my master's degree was rather like that. I studied via distance learning as I could not take time off work and at first completing all the courses seemed an insurmountable challenge. However, I tackled one course at a time and just kept ticking them off, and eventually, three and a half years later, I completed the whole degree course. For these 'long haul' challenges there are techniques which can help you keep on track and which can help keep you motivated.

Huge projects

The techniques I describe have been used on huge projects such as building the channel tunnel or launching a space satellite. These large projects will be broken down into a myriad of smaller tasks with intermediate goals and detailed tasks for the huge teams contributing to the project. Although they will use detailed analysis to plan the project, the basic techniques are the same as in this book. The people who manage these projects aren't superhuman – they just follow tried and tested approaches. You don't need complicated computer systems – or even any computer systems at all. There are special packages which are used for managing projects but you don't need them and I will not be referring to them.

Even small jobs will benefit

The good news is that these tools work just as well with small projects and will help make sure that when you're planning any task you don't forget anything and you achieve what you set out to do. I have a tendency to rush into things and taking time to plan, even if it's only a very short space of time, will ensure everything goes smoothly. If you've decided to go out for a picnic, it'll help you plan what to do, so that you don't end up only getting away for 10 minutes, or leaving the sandwiches at home, or forgetting something to cope with any rain showers.

The same approach can be used for virtually any task

The approach can be used for any sort of task in any walk of life. I use the techniques each time I compete in a triathlon. The captain of my running club, a qualified coach, has said it's important to break even a single race down into bite-size chunks so that a marathon becomes two separate 10-mile races with a 10-kilometre race on the end. A complete marathon can seem too big a challenge, but broken down it becomes much more manageable.

You can use it at home, at work or in your hobbies or pastimes. At home you might be decorating the front room, organising the family holiday or planning your daughter's wedding. I've used it to plan house moves, extend my house, plan my own wedding and a whole range of parties and social activities.

At work I've used it to launch a plumbing company, restructure a whole department and develop a training programme, as well as for a wide range of projects in construction from installing new pipelines to building an extension to a sewage works. In my leisure time, I've used the techniques to start breeding alpacas, complete the London to Brighton Bike Ride, train and compete in triathlons and plan a jazz concert. For me, these techniques are almost second nature and I plan things automatically using the techniques in this book.

No challenge too large

The times when these techniques really come into their own are for the large challenges which seem so huge you don't know where to start. Hundreds of years ago, Lao Tzu famously said "A journey of a thousand miles begins with a single step". This is still very true. This book will help you work out what the first step should be. Then, once you've made the first step, you continue step by step until you realise that you're well on your way and the huge challenge is not so insurmountable after all.

You're capable of much more than you imagine

Often people feel they are not up to a task. The size of it may appear overwhelming. This is something that most people feel, even the ones who ooze self-confidence. Everyone is capable of far more than they imagine and if you finish one big task the next one really does start to look more manageable. When I first took part in the London to Brighton Bike Ride, I never thought I could cycle over 50 miles in one go. However, I built up to the distance gradually and on the day my friend and I focused on reaching the next refreshment stop – and then the next and the next until we were on the outskirts of Brighton with no more hills to climb and a steady downhill slope to the sea. I will admit that the fact that each refreshment stop was filled with wonderful homemade cakes baked by local charities and youth organisations made focusing on each one quite a pleasurable task!

Once I'd completed the ride I went on to complete even longer bike rides and then went on a cycling holiday where I was cycling 50 miles a day for a whole fortnight. I had progressed from feeling that a couple of miles' cycling was a major excursion to someone who could cycle long distances and enjoy it. In the same way, if you complete one challenge you will find that it helps you to go on and complete others, as well as giving you the confidence to continue to tackle even more.

Avoid problems by planning

Some people never tackle a challenge because they are scared of making mistakes. The techniques in this book will help you avoid the worst problems by carefully planning what to do and how to avoid the things which could go wrong. Still, it is inevitable that occasionally, even with the best planning, things may go wrong. If this happens, comfort yourself with the fact that you will have learnt valuable lessons.

Even mistakes can be put to use

In one triathlon I managed to miss the fact that there was a large bar over the entrance to the car park. My bicycle was on my roof rack and I was only aware there was a problem when I heard a large crash above the car. It turned out that my bicycle was completely wrecked. I certainly learnt a few lessons that time. The thing I was most upset about was not the damage to the bike (it was an old one anyway), but the fact that I could not compete in the race. I spoke to the race organisers and they agreed to allow my friend to start early so that I was able to use her bike when she had finished the bike leg. I was so pleased to be racing and so determined not to let my friend down that I came in with the best time of the year. The disaster had been turned into success.

The inventor Thomas Edison had to make hundreds of light bulbs as each time he tried to use one, it shattered. Finally, he managed to find a design which worked. When people asked him how he coped with so much failure and how he kept himself going with so many problems, he replied, "Failure? What failure? I've just been working on a 999-step research project".

Optimise your resources

Even if you are quite happy tackling large projects, the approaches described in the book will help ensure that you minimise your problems and make the most of all your resources. They will ensure that you use your time, effort and money in the most effective way and that achieving your goals is done in the easiest possible way.

These techniques allow anyone to succeed

In Chapter 1 we looked at the benefits of tackling large projects and why people should not keep avoiding things because they seem too large or frightening to tackle. There is every incentive to have a go and these techniques should allow anyone to do that and succeed.

Key Points

▼ *This book uses tried and tested approaches*

▼ *The approaches will adapt to any task or project*
   - *large or small*
   - *in work or personal life*
   - *long- or short-term*

▼ *The keys to success are good planning and dividing the task into 'bite-size chunks'*

▼ *The approaches will optimise your resources and minimise your problems*

CHAPTER THREE

Develop a Big Picture

The power of pictures

The first thing you need to do before any detailed planning starts is to develop a picture of what you want to do – something that represents finishing your task successfully.

I'm sure you've heard the saying 'A picture speaks a thousand words'. Pictures are indeed very powerful and you can make pictures work for you when you're putting together your plan. In this chapter we'll look at why it's a good idea to have a picture of what things will be like when you've finished and how to do that in the most effective way.

A prompt to creativity

Pictures can work on the mind in all sorts of ways. Have you ever bought a car and then started seeing lots of the same make on every road you drive down? The make didn't suddenly become more popular – it's just that your mind makes connections. This could be useful in all sorts of ways. Maybe you've a picture of a party you want to hold but you can't think of how to provide the necessary catering equipment. With a strong picture always available in your mind, you may see something which can be adapted – which you'd never have thought of without that picture. This worked with me when I decided to organise a waffle stall to raise funds for charity. The only problem was that I couldn't think how to mix the huge quantity of batter that I'd need. However, on a trip round a DIY shop I spotted a paint-stirrer attachment and various plastic containers. With the aid of an electric drill to drive the paint stirrer, I had no problem mixing the batter and stored it in a big plastic bin.

Visualisation works

I've used the technique myself to great effect in my work. I was the first lady competitor in a national competition for the water industry where manual workers had to make a connection on to a water main charged up with water under pressure. The technique was quite complicated and involved various operations with a ratchet which had to be turned in the right direction. Unfortunately, I wasn't given much opportunity to practise for real – water pipes are expensive and all the guys were hogging the practice rig. I went over and over the operation in my mind and it worked. Although I'd only managed to run through the operation a couple of times, I went through it perfectly and matched the time of the winner of the first male competition.

Develop a clear picture

Napoleon Hill, who carried out a study of the richest businessmen in the USA at the start of the last century, identified the huge impact this had on the businessmen. One thing they all had in common was a clear picture of what they wanted to achieve.

He said, "Thoughts are things, and powerful things at that, when they are mixed with definiteness of purpose, persistence and a burning desire for their translation into ... material objects." He went on to say, "Whatever the mind of man can conceive and believe it can achieve."

Having a clear picture will also help you develop the rest of your plans. It will help you decide what to do and, just as importantly, what not to do. It will help ensure that you don't get side-tracked into doing extra things that perhaps other people think are a good idea but which maybe are not so important to you.

Daydream

So how do you build your picture? Daydreaming is a good start. This might seem strange in a book about action but it's true. Start by thinking about what you want to achieve. You may be very good at imagining, but if you're not, don't worry. You may not have a very strong picture at first but keep thinking and gradually add to the picture. What end point do you want to achieve? It may be a wonderful wedding reception with everyone having a great time and your daughter looking really radiant. Maybe it's a new boss welcoming you to your new job, shaking you by the hand and wishing you well. Perhaps it's the finishing line at the end of a marathon with all the crowds around clapping and cheering.

Even if you start with a very hazy image, even if you can't see the colours or only see part of the scene, keep building it up and adding detail and colours so that it becomes more vivid. The stronger it becomes, the more it will be fixed in your brain. If it's the wedding reception then think of the guests. Who will be there? Picture your friends and relations one by one. Make sure they are all smiling and happy. What will the bride and groom look like? Imagine their happy faces and what they are wearing. Where will it be held? What will the table decorations look like? Will there be food and what will that look like?

Pictures help to build champions

This technique is used a lot by sports coaches. Successful sports men and women will picture every part of a race in detail including winning the race. They will make it so real it becomes a self-fulfilling prophesy. Trials where this technique has been used with some sportsmen but not with others have shown that the ones imagining success rather than just training their body did better, and demonstrate the power of the mind. It's a great way to overcome all those niggling voices that can stop you in your tracks. Of course, the niggling voices may be difficult to overcome at first. If they are tending to get in the way, then just relax and tell yourself you're playing 'let's pretend'. If you keep imagining, the picture will gradually become more and more fixed in your mind and the niggling voices will die away.

I use the techniques in triathlons. When I started competing in races, I just imagined finishing. At school I would do anything to get out of games and had never competed in any sport since so this was going to be a real challenge. A sprint triathlon would mean well over an hour and a half of hard exercise. The longest I'd managed was a few minutes of active disco dancing. Still, I kept building up the picture of running up to the finish line. I went down to the race location the week before and that helped me to imagine the finish line in even more detail. I pictured the sports field where the race ended with a big finish banner. I imagined the supporters encouraging everyone on. My friend who had persuaded me to have a go would be there (she was bound to finish first!) encouraging me, along with her husband. That picture stayed with me and kept me going as I plodded up and down the swimming pool and ran along the towpath near my house in training. It also kept me going during the actual race when my legs felt like jelly and all I wanted to do was sit down. Now I know I can finish a triathlon, I start imagining the time clock above the finish with my target time on it. I picture each section of the race in my mind, imagining it all going smoothly.

Add the other senses

Once you have a picture in your mind then start adding the other senses. Add the sounds. If it's a party, what music will be playing? Imagine the sounds of people chatting and laughing happily. If there are toasts, imagine everyone joining in the toast and clinking glasses. If you want a new job, imagine your new colleagues saying hello. For my triathlon I imagined the crowds cheering everyone on and my friends shouting my name. 'Come on Jo, you're nearly there. Well done. Great stuff.' There may be smells you want to imagine – the flowers on the table, the smell of champagne. In my case, the smell of the newly-mown grass on the playing field where the organisers have the finish line. Then think about tastes. Again, champagne may come into it or perhaps your favourite meal. In a triathlon it's the taste of sports drink and a banana at the finishing line – there's usually a big box of them at the end of any triathlon.

Once you've got the sights, sounds, smells and tastes fixed, then you need to think about your feelings. There are two parts to this. Firstly think about the physical feelings you may have on the day: shaking hands with the new boss, kissing your daughter and new son-in-law, hugging your friends at the end of the marathon. Put these feelings into the picture. I imagined the feel of my feet running across that final playing field and, ever hopeful, my lungs bursting as I went for a sprint finish.

Add emotions

Even more importantly, think about your emotions at the time. How do you want to feel? You may want to feel joyful, bubbly. In the case of a new job, you may want to feel relaxed and confident. In the case of my triathlon, I wanted to feel pleased and happy. I also wanted to feel the confidence which finishing a sports event like that would give me. I knew I would feel tired but I didn't think about that too much, I just focused on the positives.

Build the picture in your mind

With all the senses brought into your picture, it's time now to build up that picture in your mind. Whenever you can, bring the picture up and, if you are somewhere where you can relax and close your eyes, really focus on the picture and on your emotions. Make those emotions as strong as you can. A good time to do this is each night just before you go to sleep. Just relax and bring the picture up in your mind with all the senses and emotions. That way your mind will have a positive picture as you sleep and your subconscious can work overnight.

Be selfish

One important thing to remember is that you are doing this for yourself. Even if you want to arrange something for someone else – for instance, the example of a wedding or maybe a house move, getting an elderly relative into sheltered accommodation – make the picture yours. What emotions do you want to feel? What do you want to see? This is where it pays to be really selfish. What you do you want to get out of the project? It's important you are really clear about this. By all means, imagine your daughter's happy face at the wedding, but think about how that will make you feel.

It may be you are doing something for charity. However, the important focus for you at this stage is to think about how that will make you feel. What will the activity look like from your point of view? If you are arranging a charity ball, how do you want to feel at the end of the evening? Of course you want other people to have enjoyed themselves, but you may want to feel relaxed and satisfied yourself. It may be you want to feel the satisfaction of having contributed to something you believe in. My next door neighbour organised an amazing garage sale, complete with a celebrity opening, refreshments and a children's play area. The satisfaction she got from raising hundreds of pounds for a charity she believed in so strongly was more than ample reward for her.

It might be you want the incentive of a charity event to achieve something for yourself. Many people enter sponsored sporting and activity events as a spur to help them to get fit or develop a new skill. The first time I entered the London to Brighton Bike Ride, although I did collect sponsors, my motivation was to improve my bike riding and have a great day out. I'm pleased to say that I achieved both, and it fired a love of cycling which has stayed with me ever since. The nice thing about many activities which will help other people is that you can get a lot out of them yourself, so it may well be possible to have some objectives for yourself as well as for other people.

What do you really want?

Some people find it difficult to sort out what they want from what they think they should do. Many of us have a strong sense of duty and have been taught from an early age to support our spouse, our children or our boss. Thinking what we want ourselves can be a little alien. If you struggle to divide what you think is the right thing to do from what you really want, try this exercise. Work with a friend and tell him or her about the outcome you have imagined. They then ask 'What do you really want?' Answer the question and then they must ask again 'What do you really want?' If the two of you keep working away, sooner or later you will get to an answer which you realise is what you really want in your heart of hearts. You'll know when you reach that point – you'll feel a warmth and satisfaction thinking about it that you did not get earlier. If you don't have a close friend or relative you feel comfortable doing this with, try it on your own. Writing down the question and the answer may help clarify your thoughts.

My wedding

This exercise helped me sort out what I really wanted for my own wedding. Before my husband asked me to marry him, I'd had vague thoughts about white weddings with a big party. Then after he'd proposed to me, planning a wedding was a reality.

Initially I still thought of a big 'do' but when I thought about what I wanted and kept answering the question 'What do I really want?' I came up with quite a short list of requirements which were the most important to me:

▼ *I wanted my husband to have a wonderful day*

▼ *I wanted to enjoy every minute of the day myself*

▼ *I wanted to feel that our wedding was special and unique*

▼ *I wanted a wedding which would bring back wonderful memories for the rest of my life*

I really wasn't too worried by where the wedding should be and, as I knew my husband really didn't want a large wedding, if I was going to satisfy the first requirement then it would have to be a small wedding. We ended up getting married on the island of South Georgia near the Antarctic and our wedding fulfilled every one of my four requirements and, as far as I was concerned, was truly perfect. I was so glad I had spent time thinking about what it was that I really wanted.

The subconscious can be very helpful

That's an example of how your subconscious can come up with answers that you might not have thought of without a clear understanding of what you are looking for. With my requirements for my wedding firmly lodged in my brain, I was free to spot a possible solution – one which I had never contemplated before. Of course, there was still a lot to organise, but I had the end picture and a clear view of how I wanted to feel at the end of the day.

Make the picture permanent

Once you've got a clear picture of what you want to achieve from your big task, you need to make that more permanent. You can make this fun and use whatever method suits you best. There are four main ways you can do this and which one you choose is entirely a matter of preference. You may even go for more than one which will help establish the picture in your mind even more firmly.

A word picture

The first option is to write a description. The key is to write something which means something to you. Sit down, clear your mind and then bring up your picture. Make it bright and engaging as I described before and then write down what you see. Use plenty of description words and put in as much detail as you possibly can. Don't worry if you don't think of everything at once – you can build on the initial description and keep adding to it as you think of things. Here's my description of my wedding:

> *The sun is shining, the air is clean and fresh. The church bells are ringing. Neil and I come out of the church holding each other's hands. I see my shining wedding ring on my hand. Neil has a huge smile on his face and he looks very relaxed. I feel so happy I could almost burst and I grin from ear to ear. I feel so proud of my wonderful husband. I am wearing a wonderful outfit which makes me feel like a princess. We hug and kiss. Our witnesses come out and give us each a hug.*

When I first wrote this I couldn't think exactly what I wanted to wear, but I added that in later as my ideas crystallised.

Record the image

If you find writing difficult but still like the idea of a description, why not record it? Again, you can use any method – computers and iPods usually have facilities. You can play your description to yourself in any odd moments – in the car, cooking or just before you go to sleep.

Draw a picture

If you find pictures easier to produce than words, why not draw a picture? Again, it doesn't have to be an artistic masterpiece; if you can't draw people, use stick men. Again, keep adding to the picture and make it as detailed as you want. I am absolutely hopeless at drawing, but I did a picture of my wedding dream. You'll see that artistic ability is definitely NOT required!

Figure 3.1 My wedding picture

Use other people's pictures

If you don't want to draw, you can always put a collage together using pictures from magazines and any other items to build up a scene of what you want. It might be useful to buy a specialist magazine to find the pictures you want. For a sporting event, there are plenty of specialist magazines or for a special occasion try the celebrity magazines. To make the collage more real, use photographs of your face and those of your friends and relatives. This is easier with the advent of

Figure 3.3 The collage for my first Olympic-distance triathlon

digital photographs. I did this when I wanted to complete my first Olympic-distance triathlon. I cut out a photo from a report of the event from the previous year, which had taken place in perfect weather, and pasted my face on to one of the competitors. That took minimal effort but provided me with a real picture for the event.

Keep on looking or listening

Once you've completed the picture, be it a word picture, a recording, a drawing or a collage, you need to put the picture to good use. Put it somewhere you will see it regularly. If you are happy for everyone to see the picture, then put it somewhere for the whole family to see. This can be very powerful; if your whole family knows what you want to do, they can share your picture. This can be a tremendously powerful motivator in itself and does ensure that everyone agrees on what you're trying to do.

Stick it on the fridge, the mantelpiece, above the TV or on the bathroom mirror. If it's a recording, have it somewhere where you can play it regularly. Keep it on a CD in the car, a Dictaphone by the bed or load it on to an MP3 player.

A private option

Of course, there may be good reasons why you want to keep the picture to yourself. In that case, you can keep it in the car, in your handbag or briefcase or even in the potting shed! The key is to make sure that you see the picture regularly. This will keep you on track and ensure that tackling the big task is at the forefront of your mind.

Make your dream come true

If you follow these instructions, you'll be surprised how ideas come to you. The picture will keep you working in the right direction. It will help you to pick yourself up should you find you've hit some problems and will help your dream to come true. You'll believe that your dream will come true and that is more than half the battle.

Key Points

▼ *Before you do anything, picture the final result*

▼ *Visualisation is a very powerful tool*

▼ *Involve all the senses – sound, smell, taste, feelings as well as sight*

▼ *Make your picture permanent*
   -write a description
   -draw a sketch
   -use magazines and photos

▼ *Keep referring to your picture*

CHAPTER FOUR

Expand the picture

What will success look like?

Once you've developed a really strong picture of what you want to achieve with your project, there's still a bit more work to make sure you've considered everything about your end point. One important question to be answered is 'What will success look like?' This might mean that you need to add some extra scenes into your picture. Suppose you are planning a party. You might have an idea of how you want it to go, but what do you want your guests to think? Would a successful party include avoiding upsetting the neighbours? Would it mean getting the house back to a clean and tidy state by lunchtime on the following day?

Other people's viewpoints

Now you've thought about things from your point of view, you might need to think about things from other people's points of view. If you want them to be happy with the outcome, what sort of things would they consider important? What would your spouse want, your children, your friends and neighbours? If it's a work project, think about who needs to be involved at work amongst your colleagues. What would your boss consider successful and would that be different from your idea of success? A successful triathlon for me includes one in which my husband doesn't get too bored, has a bacon butty, a cup of coffee and a read of the Sunday papers while he's waiting for me to finish, which might mean I need to check he's remembered to take enough cash on top of my own preparations.

Ask other people

It may be useful to ask people for their views on what a successful outcome would include. It may not be what you would assume. Maybe you thought your neighbours didn't want to be disturbed by a party you're planning, but in fact they'd love to come and join in the fun. Maybe your boss is not so worried that some new procedures are written down, but that everyone in the department feels involved in developing them. It's useful to write down what success looks like from different viewpoints. When I managed the merger of two companies, I wrote down what each senior manager from the two companies wanted and what was important to each of them for a successful merger. It raised several points I would not have thought about on my own and, by talking to each of them about what they wanted, it made sure that they all felt involved and consulted.

Costs

You may need to think about the cost when considering what success looks like. Managing projects with a tight budget can be very challenging but it can be fun as well and can inspire you to improvise to avoid some unnecessary costs. In the case of the party, you might have a budget for the food and drink so that you have to be creative with your cooking to provide good food that doesn't cost too much. Your success factor might allow for a bigger budget with outside caterers and less stress for you. I went to a party recently at a friend's house and she had arranged for a couple of people to come in for a few hours to serve the drinks and food so that she could have time to talk to her friends. It cost her more but added to her enjoyment. There's no right or wrong answer – you've got to decide what is right for you.

The power of questions

When considering your plans, never underestimate the power of questions. Rudyard Kipling summed it up in a short poem.

I keep six honest serving men
They taught me all I knew
Their names are what and where and when
And why and how and who.

If you think about each of the questions, they may help you strengthen your picture. You've already done a lot of work on the 'what'. 'What will be the end point? What is your and others' definition of success? What do you need to do?' and 'What resources will you need?' will be covered later. Some projects may require a special location – where is the right location? A typical project where this is important is a wedding. Choosing the location may well dictate many other decisions. In my case, this was definitely true as getting married on the edge of the Antarctic Circle on the island of South Georgia dictated all sorts of other decisions, like what to wear and who to invite.

Motivation

Thinking about 'why' will lead you to think about your motivation. Understanding your motivation can help keep you going – or even get you started. Think about why you want to take on this challenge, and why others might be willing to help you. In my case with this book, it was meeting so many people who seemed scared to act and wanting to help them that has spurred me on, along with the feeling that I had a good idea for a book and would be really gutted if I saw a similar book produced by someone else. The 'how' we'll come to in the next chapter.

People

'Who needs to be involved?' is also an important question and that question is answered in Chapter 7. If you're organising an event, however, it may be useful to think about who the target audience will be, who is likely to come. Is it the people from your village, is it friends, is it family, is it everyone who enjoys a Christmas Panto?

Timing

The timing of when a project needs to be completed can be critical. A celebration may need to be on a certain day. You may need to gain a qualification by a certain date. If you have flexibility with timing that can make things easier, although it can sometimes make motivation more difficult. I had no deadline for completing this book and it lay unstarted for several years!

Getting started

In fact, getting started can often be the biggest challenge of the whole project. If you have a good idea or a burning ambition but just can't seem to get started, then it's worthwhile taking time to think about what is stopping you. It may be worthwhile writing down all the reasons why you haven't started. Once you've done that, find an argument to counter each excuse.

Finding time

One of the most frequent excuses is that you don't have time. We all only have 24 hours in a day and 365 days in a year. However, different people achieve different things with their time and, rather than lack of time, it tends to be a matter of priorities. If you really want to carry out a particular project, then you will find the time. As I type this, we're having the first sunny weather we've had for days and I'd much rather be out on my bicycle. However, if I don't spend the time on the book, it'll never get written. As my motivation to finish the book is greater than my desire for a bike ride, I keep typing.

Sometimes time can disappear without necessarily doing anything we really like. Are you spending too much time watching television, although you complain about the quality of the programmes? Do you have an extra 15 minutes' doze after the alarm goes? Is the house absolutely immaculate and could it, in fact, just be reasonably clean and tidy? Are you just too tired, in which case do you need to think about getting fitter first before you take on something new? Achieving that would spur you on to tackle an additional project. If you really want to do something you will make time to do it.

Procrastination

Sometimes you may just never get round to something. Procrastination is quite literally a waste of time – and it can be very stressful. Often it can be caused by fear. People put things off because they are worried that their shortcomings will be revealed or that it will be too difficult or even painful – either physically or emotionally. If you take a deep breath and just get stuck in you'll probably be amazed at what you achieve. Often people find things to do to avoid doing the task which appears more difficult. This is sometimes referred to as displacement activity. My husband always knows when I've a difficult task to tackle as the house is always at its cleanest and tidiest. Think carefully about how you are spending your time and if you think there's some displacement activity, make your mind up to take the first step right away and then just do it. The feeling once you've taken that first step will be well worth it and the chances are that, whatever the task was, it will be a lot less difficult than you thought.

Shortly after buying my first house, which required that I used all my savings and had the maximum mortgage I could afford, I discovered that the roof over the bay window was rotten. I had no money to bring in builders so decided to do it myself. Starting that project was terrifying – I had never tackled any major building, just some small DIY jobs. However, the rot would not get any better and I knew the longer I left it, the worse it would get. A bank holiday was coming up and I resolved that as long as it didn't rain I would start then. Once I had pulled away the rotten timbers I was committed and, as I worked over that summer, I grew more and more confident about the work and since then have tackled much larger building jobs. That first step was the most difficult part of the work.

Start with something easy

In some cases, it might be worthwhile deciding on a small but easy step to get started. A major goal can seem too daunting so committing to a small step can be much more manageable. If you keep making those small steps forward then eventually you will reach your goal. Each action builds momentum and confidence so that the project becomes easier and easier.

In my mid thirties, I decided to study for a management degree, an MBA. As I did not feel I could take time off work, I opted for a distance learning course, which required me to study entirely on my own. The first lot of study material arrived in November. Come December I still had not started. In fact, I had not even opened the parcel. I made up my mind that on New Year's Day I would open all the packages and sort everything out and read the material. I felt that was not such a difficult task and I would not worry about studying or completing my assignments. It made a huge difference and the next weekend I felt ready to have a go at my first assignment and then I was up and running. As I completed each assignment I found the studying easier and easier and I even missed the studying when I finished the course.

Tell someone else

Another way to get over the problem of prevarication is to tell someone else of your plans. That was how I got over the first few hurdles of competing in triathlons. I told my work colleague that I would compete with her in a race. I was committed. She was not going to let me escape and that spurred me on to take swimming lessons so that at least I had a chance of swimming the whole distance. I've told several people that I'm writing this book and they ask me how it's going from time to time. As I hate lying and don't want to be embarrassed by saying I've done nothing, it makes a strong incentive for me to keep working – even when it's warm and sunny outside.

Six coloured hats

So far, you've thought about what you want to achieve and identified all the different factors which need to be met to gain success. There is one technique which will help ensure that you have thought of everything you need to cover. This was developed by Edward de Bono who investigated how the mind works. He identified six different ways of looking at a problem and suggested that each could be represented by a colour. To help a person focus on each aspect, he suggested you think about each of these as putting on a hat of a different colour. If you concentrate on the aspect represented by that colour hat, this may help you think of things you may have missed. People tend to have one or two approaches to looking at a problem which come easier to them than others. However, to really think about a project you need to think in all six ways.

What the colours represent

The first way is the white hat. This way of thinking focuses on the facts. What do you know about the project? What information do you have? This is the blank piece of paper to be filled with facts and figures. The red hat, the colour of fire, is quite different – what are the emotions involved? What are people's opinions and feelings on a subject? The yellow 'sunshine' hat thinks of all the positives in a situation such as 'Why will it work?' 'What good will come out of it?' while the black hat thinks of all the negatives, just like a judge's robe. The green hat, the colour of plants, represents creativeness and new approaches, alternative ways of solving problems. Finally, the blue hat, the colour of sky, thinks about the big picture, how everything fits together in an overall process.

Figure 4.1 Six Thinking Hats

If we look at how I used these hats when thinking about building an extension to my last house, I've listed some of the issues brought out by each hat.

White hat – facts

▼ *The current house has no spare room*
▼ *The sitting room is too small for my needs*
▼ *There is a huge garden*
▼ *I have saved up enough money to cover the estimated cost of an extension*

Red hat – emotions

▼ *I feel nervous at tackling my largest building project yet*
▼ *I enjoy making a house just as I want it*
▼ *I don't like the layout of the house as it is*

Black hat – negatives

▼ *I don't know any local builders*
▼ *I don't know any local architects*
▼ *I don't have planning permission*

▼ *There are lots of cowboy builders around*

▼ *There will be brick dust in everything while the work's being done*

▼ *I'll have nowhere to put anything while the work is being done*

▼ *It will use up all my spare savings*

Yellow hat – positives

▼ *The house will be worth more when it's finished*

▼ *I can design the house to be just as I want it*

▼ *I can have a big kitchen with a view of the garden*

▼ *I can have a heated floor in the kitchen*

▼ *I will be able to fit in a lodger which will bring in a regular income*

Green hat – creative

▼ *If I put in an entirely new entrance at the side of the house it will all work much better*

▼ *I could design the house on Feng Shui principles*

▼ *If I designed the layout I could get a building technician to draw up the details*

▼ *If I put a roof light in the back of the house it would be much lighter*

▼ *I could put in solar heating*

Blue hat – the whole picture

▼ *Now I've settled into my new job I could take on this new project*

▼ *I have several past building projects which will stand me in good stead*

▼ *The whole project should not take more than a year*

▼ *The building department at work may be able to give me some contacts*

This way of focusing on different ways of thinking at a time makes sure that all the different aspects of a project are taken into consideration and helps you think about aspects you might otherwise have missed. If you're a born optimist then perhaps black hat thinking may be more difficult, whilst a very emotional person may find it helpful to think in white hat mode and try to just focus on the facts.

Using the six hats approach can make planning fun, especially if you work with friends or family. One friend I knew even turned up to a meeting with sets of six coloured baseball caps to help us remember how we were supposed to be thinking. Planning doesn't have to be a dry, dusty activity and putting some effort into developing your plans will play dividends in the long run.

Key Points

▼ *Add other information to your vision of the end result*
- *other people's views*
- *costs*
- *who needs to be involved*

▼ *Ask yourself questions to make sure you've covered everything*

▼ *Getting started may be the most difficult step*
- *understand your motivation*
- *think about time commitment*
- *start with something easy*

▼ *Tell someone what you're planning and get them to nag you*

▼ *Edward de Bono's Six Thinking Hats will help ensure you've thought of everything*

CHAPTER FIVE

Build a route plan

Break it into bite-size chunks

So far, you've thought a lot about your project but in this chapter you will really start to understand how to cut up the elephant. It's all very well to say divide it up into bite-size chunks, but how big should they be, how do you organise them and keep track of them all? This chapter will explain what to do.

Involve friends and family

Although you can do this stage on your own, you can also rope in other people – your family, friends or colleagues. For my wedding, I sat down with my husband. For the company merger I managed, I worked with managers from the two companies. It does work better if you choose people you like and with whom you get on well. Obviously there was no problem with my husband, but I did choose my colleagues carefully. This session should be fun so you need people you can laugh and joke with. If you do this on your own, then I suggest you go through the exercise once and then come back to it after a break to see if you can find anything you have forgotten. For the triathlon I worked on my own, but did check things with the friend from work who had talked me into the race. Most of my friends and family would have thought I was totally mad so I left them out. However, if you do involve people close to you, it will help them understand what you are tackling and this will have lots of benefits. They can check how you're progressing, support you if the motivation flags and make allowances for you if other things in your life take a lower priority for a while.

Make it fun

The more fun you can make the session the better. You could turn it into a party with food, drinks and energising music. What you will need are lots of post-it notes and pens (felt tips are particularly good) plus a large piece of paper somewhere you can stick the notes so that everyone can see them. Attach it to a blank piece of wall or lay it out on a large table or the floor. The piece of paper needs to be as large as possible – a whole sheet of wrapping paper is about the minimum size, although several stuck together would be better. You could use a length of lining paper or brown parcel-wrapping paper, or even some wallpaper, providing it has a reasonably plain pattern which you can write on.

Get the brain cells working

A good way to start the session is an exercise which gets everyone into the mood and which starts people thinking creatively. Pass round an everyday item – I've used a pen, a wooden spoon and a paper clip – and ask people to come up with new uses for the item. At my sessions, the pen could be used to stir coffee, make holes in the soil for seeds, a ruler to draw a straight line and a weight on a piece of string as a plumb bob. The paper clip has been used to clean nails, hang things up and connected to others to make a necklace. The wooden spoon has been used as fuel for a fire, stuck in a crack in a garden wall as a bird feeder or as a drum stick. It really doesn't matter what people say. Keep going round and round everyone there so that people have used up all the obvious ideas and are starting to come up with some fairly wacky ones. This should set the mood nicely and make sure people's minds are working and they feel comfortable making suggestions, however outlandish.

Explain the project

Now it's your turn to explain to people what you want to achieve with the project you have in mind. If you have drawn a picture or put together a collage, then show it to everyone and if possible put it somewhere everyone can see it. Go through what you want to get out of the project and all the thoughts you have had about timing, costs and what success will mean to the different people involved.

Brainstorm

'Brainstorm' what you need to do

When everyone understands the project, ask them all to think of everything that needs to be done to achieve the end target. These can be large jobs or small jobs and this can be done as a 'brainstorm'. This is just a way of letting people think of everything without interruption so that they can get into the flow of things and just allow the ideas to come.

Ask everyone to write each job or activity on a separate post-it note – one job per post-it. Allow some time while people just write. Once one or two have run out of ideas, got bored or if you spot someone just staring into space, go round the group and ask each person to read out an action and then stick it on to the large piece of paper you prepared. While this is going on, try to stick with a few rules:

▼ *No discussion*
▼ *Any action is valid*
▼ *Anyone is welcome to write additional ideas at any time*

You may find some interesting ideas come out of the session, but remember the rules. Of course having a good laugh at some ideas is certainly allowed. In Figure 5.1 I've shown the post-it notes collected for a barbeque I planned.

Eventually everyone will run out of ideas and you may get to suggestions for actions which really aren't needed or are so creative they are totally bizarre. Now is the time to call a halt. It may be a good time for a break and to refill glasses or cups.

Figure 5.1 Photo of barbeque post-it notes

Sort the post-it notes

Once everyone has had a break, go back to the collection of post-its. Let everyone look at all of them for a while. After a few minutes you'll start to see ones which are linked. For instance, if you're planning a party, there might be some actions related to catering, others to invitations and others to accommodation. Start re-arranging the post-its so that similar activities are linked. Once you've got post-its grouped, start to look at the groups critically. Do you have any actions which are duplicated? If you do, then throw away any duplications so that you just have one post-it for one action. In some cases, one action may be a combination of several actions. 'Organise the catering' could require 'deciding what to eat, buying the food, cooking it and serving it up'. In some cases, there might be several ways of doing things; for instance, with the catering, an alternative might be to find local caterers, obtain sample menus, choose caterer, hire caterer. In this case you might want an additional action of 'decide whether to do catering yourself or get in outside caterers'.

The party post-it notes in Figure 5.1 were sorted as shown in figure 5.2 after we'd gone through this exercise. You can see we identified one group of activities all related to logistics, another all related to planning the event and a further one all related to food and cooking.

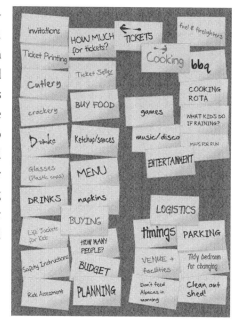

Figure 5.2 Photo of sorted post-it notes

Put the post-it notes in date order

Once you've checked all the notes for duplications, omissions or composite actions, rearrange the groups in lines of related activities. Check for the order of the actions. For instance, in the post-its for the barbeque, there is one which says 'decide the price of the tickets' and another which says 'print invitations'. Clearly the price and the timings of the event must both be decided before printing the notices or invitations. The invitations or notices telling people about the barbeque need to be sent out before the tickets can be sold.

Clearly there is an order in which these activities should be done. Move the post-its around until the order of the activities makes sense.

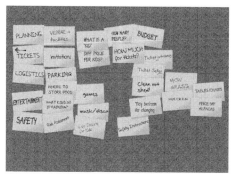

Figure 5.3 Photo of post-it notes in date order

Identify chains of action

As you rearrange the post-its, you'll start to get some chains of actions which need to be carried out one after the other, and other actions which could be carried out at any time. Start arranging the post-its in the chains, with one chain of actions above another. Everyone needs to be thinking 'What must be done before task X can be finished?' 'Can task Y be done in parallel with task Z?' This way you'll start to see that some tasks are dependent on others. In some cases, like the example of sending out the invitations I gave before, several activities will need to be completed before one can send out the invitations.

Unidentified tasks may also come to light and new post-its can be added at any time. For example, 'hire a photographer' might actually need additional activities like 'make list of local photographers', 'obtain quotes from photographers' and 'choose best quote'.

Develop a map of how you'll get to the end

Eventually you'll have all the tasks listed in lines of activity as we did in Figure 5.3. Put in arrows flowing from one action to another to show what must be done in what order. Arrange them so that as you move from left to right on the piece of paper, the actions are

Figure 5.4 Photo of finished action plan

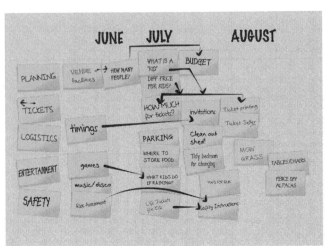

roughly in date order with any actions which must all be finished before something else can be done to the left of that dependent action. Figure 5.4 shows how my party post-it notes finished up. You now have the outline of an action plan or route plan. It's like a map showing you how to get from where you are now to where you want to be.

Capture your plan and display it

If it's quite a small project, this may be enough to show you what to do. If you have the space, you can leave the sheet of paper up on a wall where you can see it and this will help you work out what you have to do. However, a warning – post-it notes can curl up and drop off the paper; long strips of sticky tape can prevent this. Of course, not everyone has room to do that so you may need to copy it on to a smaller piece of paper. If you are good with computers you could use a simple standard system to draw out what you have prepared. This could be done using a drawing, presentation or spreadsheet package. There are bespoke project management packages such as Microsoft Project. However, these tend to be quite complicated to use and generally require some special training to use them comfortably. A good spreadsheet or drawing package can work just as well, as my examples show.

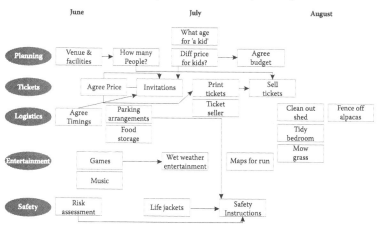

Figure 5.5 Example of barbeque project drawn up in PowerPoint

However you capture your route plan, make sure you are able to put a copy of it up somewhere where you can refer to it easily. This will be your guidance right up until you have completed the project.

Milestones may help

In some cases, a project may take several months or even years, like studying for my MBA as I described in Chapter 4. In this case you may find it helpful to identify some intermediate milestones so that you can keep track of your progress. Just as the original milestones allowed travellers to identify their progress on their journey, project milestones will also allow you track progress with your project. Even for shorter projects it can be useful to have intermediate milestones. These milestones are significant results on which subsequent actions depend.

One significant milestone for a wedding might be that the wedding venue is booked. Another might be that the invitations have been sent out. In some cases, it might be a key decision – where to hold the wedding or how many people to invite. For my MBA the milestones were quite straightforward: finishing each of the eight modules and the project. For my triathlon, one key milestone was being able to swim 400m front crawl without a break. Another was to be able to run five kilometres without stopping, after cycling for an hour. Some of the intermediate milestones will be quite obvious, although you may need to be more creative to think about others.

These milestones will help you keep track of progress as well as providing you with a good excuse for a small celebration and a pat on the back for getting so far, which is always good for the motivation.

SMART goals

A concept of 'SMART' goals may be useful here. This does not mean that the goals are particularly clever. The term SMART is an acronym where each letter stands for a particular requirement:

Specific, Measurable, Achievable, Relevant and Timed. Although this approach is more often used at work, if you have asked someone to help, the letters can be a useful reminder to you to check you have given them all the information they need.

Specific
Measurable
Achievable
Relevant
Timed

Figure 8.1 Smart Goals

Each of these requirements is explained in more detail below.

Specific and measurable

When thinking about milestones, they do need to be specific and measurable. 'Make some progress with my MBA' would not have been a very helpful milestone – it could mean reading one page in six months or completing the whole course. 'Complete the first module' is much more specific and it can be measured. When training for a sport, specific targets are very important. 'Swim faster' is not specific whilst 'complete 100m freestyle in two minutes' can be measured.

Achievable

Whilst setting ambitious targets can help people achieve amazing feats, they do need to be realistic. Starting racing triathlons at the age of forty-eight, winning the world championships was not really achievable. However, I do have the target of competing as a national team member in my age group which, whilst tough, can be achieved if I work hard.

Relevant

Relevant means the goal must relate to the task in hand. Make sure you only include milestones in your plan which will help you achieve your desired outcome. Sometimes you may want to include other things in the plan. For instance, I could set myself a target of being able to lift a certain weight in the gym. However, this is not directly relevant to improving at triathlons, although indirectly it may help. It's very easy to get distracted and if you really are tackling a major challenge you need to be very focused.

Timed

The final parameter of the SMART list is 'Timed' and means you should always say by when you will achieve a milestone. Without that it is very easy for some tasks to stretch and stretch so that you never quite finish something off. There were times when I felt that this book was rather like that. For a while my progress was rather slow until I agreed a publication date with a publisher. That then gave me the impetus to give the work priority.

Think about how long things will take

You've sorted out all the actions which need to be carried out and some intermediate milestones along the way. However, you've not thought much about how long the whole project will take from start to finish.

Look at each of the chains of actions. Work out how long each action will take to do, allowing for things like the fact that you may not be able to do some things until the weekend or during the week or on a certain evening. If we take the example of the party invitations, choosing who to invite may take an evening of going through your address book. It may take another evening to design the invitation. But in fact you're only at home two evenings a week so that will fill up one week. Printing the invitations may take a short time if you've worked up something on a computer. However, if you wanted it done by a professional printer you might need more time – say another week. Finally, sending it out might require you to address envelopes and stick on stamps – say another evening. Alternatively it might require you to print out and stick on address labels. End to end it might be sensible to allow two and a half weeks for that line of actions.

Work out timings

Go through each line of actions and work out the times. However, don't forget that you only have one pair of hands. It may be you can get help for some actions in which case allow for that, but otherwise make sure you don't overload yourself. If you're busy with the invitations, you can't be cooking up quiches to put in the freezer. You may need to decide that you need to start some actions early so that you finish early. Invitations need to go out in good time so that people can put the date in their diary. Therefore you might decide that the milestone of 'all the invitations sent out' should be reached a month before the party at the latest. However, some things may only be possible at the last minute. Arranging fresh flowers obviously needs to be done at the last possible minute, so you might put an action like that in right at the very end.

Check for 'pinch points'

Eventually you'll start to have timings for all the actions and some idea of where there are important dates to be met. Your action plan is nearly completed. However, it's useful to look through all the actions and dates and see where timings look rather tight – the pinch points. Even starting tomorrow, you might find it difficult to get everything done in time. This is the area you need to focus on the most and it may be that you'll need assistance with this chain of actions. We'll have a look at how you can get help for projects in a later chapter.

You can either put all the timings and dates on the actual sheet of paper with the post-it notes or you can add them to the drawing you completed based on your work with the post-it notes. Have a look at Figures 5.4 and 5.5 to see what I've done for my barbeque example. Here I've just added some rough timings; however, you can write on the post-its the start and finish times required. It can be useful to put the milestones in your diary.

A list of actions with target dates can also be very useful as I've compiled in figure 5.6. In this list, I've worked out timings for the actions and this is discussed more in the next chapter. I've also used the arrows from the chart with the post-it notes to work out what actions need to be completed first.

	Action	Start	Finish	Other actions to complete
	Planning			
1	Agree venue & facilities	1 June	3 June	
2	Agree budget	8 June		6, 3, 4
	Tickets			
3	Decide price	1 June	3 June	
4	Agree prices for kids	1 June	8 June	
5	Issue first notice	8 June	10 June	1, 3, 4, 10
6	Estimate numbers	3 June	8 June	
7	Find ticket seller	1 June	15 June	
8	Design & print tickets	8 June	15 June	1, 3, 4
9	Sell tickets	15 June	20 Aug	7, 8
	Logistics			
10	Agree timings	1 June	3 June	
11	Work out parking arrangements	3 June	20 Aug	6
12	Work out where to store food	3 June	20 Aug	6
13	Clean out shed	1 Aug	28 Aug	
14	Tidy bedroom	1 Aug	28 Aug	
15	Mow grass	15 Aug	28 Aug	
16	Fence off alpacas	29 Aug	29 Aug	15

Figure 5.6 Action list

Once you've added these, make sure that you keep this information readily available all the time. In the coming weeks and months you'll be able to track your progress and make sure you're keeping on target. However – that's the subject of another chapter!

Key Points

▼ *Once you've developed a strong picture of your outcome you need a route plan*

▼ *An easy way to think of all the steps is to organise a brainstorm*

▼ *A simple method is to note all the actions on post-its*

▼ *Arrange the post-its in date order*

▼ *Add some interim milestones for longer projects*

▼ *Make your milestones 'SMART'*

▼ *Make an action list*

CHAPTER SIX

Sort out what you need

Check your time limits

In Chapter 5, I explained how to put together an action plan. In this you have lines of actions with a time for each task. If you then add up all the times for each action along each line, that gives you the amount of time you will need to spend on that line of activity. If the completion date is important, you need to check that you have enough time to finish all the tasks. For this you need to check all related activities to make sure the total time they will take is within your limits.

Party music

For instance, if you're arranging a party you might have a line of activities all related to the music for the evening. The actions you identify might be:

▼ *Go through your own CDs and identify good tracks*

▼ *Copy those tracks on to your PC*

▼ *Ask friends if they have any good CDs*

▼ *Get those CDs from friends*

▼ *Copy those tracks on to your PC*

▼ *Arrange tracks into good running order*

After you've thought about the timings you might allocate the following times for each activity:

Action	Time
Go through your own CDs and identify good tracks	4 hours
Copy those tracks on to your PC	4 hours
Ask friends if they have any good CDs – send emails	5 minutes
Get those CDs from friends	4 hours
Copy those tracks on to your PC	3 hours
Arrange tracks into good running order	1 hour

Figure 6.1 Timings for actions

Allow for real life

Now, you might think it will only take 16 hours from start to finish. However, maybe you're away for the next two weekends and you only have two evenings free each week and, by the time you've got back from work, cooked the dinner and eaten it, there are only two hours left each evening before you go to bed. That means it'll take three to four weeks to do the music and that's without everything else you may need to do for the party. If you've only got five weeks to go, that might leave you rather tight on time if you've got invitations to issue, cooking to prepare and a few other tasks to complete as well.

How to make up time

So what do you do if there is not enough time? This is probably one of the most common problems that people have to deal with, but the good news is that there are several options for solving the problem. There are lots of books on time management and there are various ways they suggest you free up time.

Priorities

One option is to spend less time doing other things. Perhaps you could get some takeaways and use the time you save cooking to copy the CDs. Perhaps you could work from home one day and use the travel time you save to copy the CDs. If you really think about how you spend your time, it's amazing where you can grab some more for the important things. When I was writing this book, I told a friend who was helping me that I had not had time to write anything for several months. 'It's just a matter of priorities' she told me and she was right. You can make time for anything that's really important to you.

Multi-tasking

It may also be possible for you to do some of the work during other tasks. I wrote parts of this book in all sorts of places, grabbing odd moments whenever I could. I'd scribble ideas waiting at the dentist or waiting for my husband. I made a point of travelling by public transport and worked on my book while I was travelling. In fact, I'm on a train as I write this. That had the added bonus that it saved my ageing car from clocking up more miles and was generally more relaxing.

Thinking about the party music example, it might be possible to copy the CDs while checking emails or designing the party invitations (or even while writing a book!).

Reduce the standards

Another option is to reduce the standards or the size of the task. Do you really need all your tracks loaded on to the PC and running continuously? Perhaps people wouldn't mind if you just had a stack of your favourite CDs and whoever was nearest changed them over. Maybe if you had a shorter list you could get the work done in less time. The tracks might be repeated a few times over the course of the evening but would people enjoy the party less? This is where your hard work to define exactly what you want for your end result is important. Will the compromise in the music affect the success of the party as you defined it? Only you can answer that question but it does help you focus the mind on what's important.

Get help

It may be that you can get help. This may sound an obvious option but it's amazing how many people soldier on trying to do everything themselves when a little help would make everything so much easier. Perhaps you have a friend who loves playing around with recordings and computers. That's exactly the person to ask for help. Even if they don't take on all of the work, taking on some of it will reduce the amount you have to do. With some help it may be possible to run several tasks in parallel. In my example of party music, perhaps you could invite a friend round and while you're sorting through which tracks to use, they could be copying them on to your computer. You could even turn the evening in to a mini party with drinks, food and some of the chosen music playing away. There's more about enlisting help in the next two chapters.

Buy time

One option is to 'buy time'. By this I mean you can use money either to get someone else to do the task or to get someone to do something else to free up your own time. I've given one example of buying takeaways to free up time. Could you pay for a baby-sitter, a cleaner or a gardener to free up time? In some cases, money may buy a completely different solution. In the case of party music, you could just buy ready-made party tracks from the web and download them as they stand. Perhaps you could pay a friend or relative (or even the children of friends!) to copy the tracks. If you were feeling really rich, why not hire a disco?

Estimating timescales

Of course, all this assumes you have a good idea about how long things will take. If you're not used to estimating these things in advance, it can seem difficult to estimate timescales. However, practice makes perfect. You could start by just working out how long a task will take you – any task, even something as mundane as the shopping or walking the dog or getting ready for work. Then try working out how long everything will take over the course of a whole evening – think through what you have to do and then add up the time for each action. Once you get good at this then try a whole day. This is good practice at work as well – if you have a meeting, try estimating how long that meeting will take. It may not be in your control, and you may be thinking 'How can I estimate something which could take 10 minutes or two hours?' However, if you start consciously looking at how long things take, it will start to give you an idea of how accurate you are and how much things vary.

Avoid underestimating

If you always seem to underestimate you will need to allow for this when estimating timescales. Make sure you allow extra which will cover for your optimistic estimates. If you find that your estimates are wildly out in both directions, try to work out your thought processes. Why did you think a particular activity would take a certain time? Did you base it on previous experience, or perhaps thinking through the actions required? Do other people do things more quickly or more slowly than you do? Do you overlook part of the process or imagine difficulties which actually never occur?

Practice makes perfect

You won't always be right with your time estimates, but if you keep working on them they will become more accurate more of the time. Of course, you can't always be right and there are all sorts of ways you can allow for this. The easiest is to allow plenty of spare time but that's a luxury we often don't have. Chapter 10 will show you how to allow for things not turning out as you expect.

Money

So far, we've looked at the resource of time, but you'll probably need other things as well. One resource in which you're bound to be limited is money. We've already looked at how you can overcome some time restraints by spending money on things that are ready-made, hiring help or paying to get other things done to free up your time. However, you may need to buy or hire things directly for your project.

Estimating costs

It's important to have an idea of what everything will cost as you may need to make some choices. In the extension to my last house which I talked about in Chapter 4, I asked a friend who was a building surveyor to tell me the rough costs per metre for building house extensions to give me an idea of the overall cost. I only had limited funds so I decided to go for cheaper kitchen cabinets and then I could afford the underfloor heating, which I really wanted. I re-used the old front door and some of the windows, rather than having all new, in order to save money and stay within my budget.

For the barbeque I describe in Chapter 5, we could have hired the actual barbeque itself, but this would have meant less money to spend on food, so we borrowed a barbeque and had plenty of really good quality food.

Beg or borrow

It's a good idea to list everything you're going to need for your project. Look at each item and decide if you need to buy it or if you could hire it. If you're only going to use something once – say a fancy dress outfit or a special piece of equipment – the chances are that it will work out cheaper to hire. It may be you can borrow something and it's always worth asking around. For the barbeque example in Chapter 5, we borrowed a professional-standard barbeque from a friend who is a professional caterer.

Once I'd bought my new racing bike, I lent it to another friend at my triathlon club who was racing but didn't have a proper racing bike. I didn't mind training on my old one and it made a big difference to her, both in the times for her races and also in helping her work out what she wanted when she could afford her own bike. I also thought of the time when someone lent me her bike at a race when I'd damaged mine en route. In Chapter 8 there's advice on how to get people to do things for you and this applies just as much to getting people to lend things as getting them to provide help in other ways.

Improvise

There may also be ways in which you can improvise to avoid spending money. I've had a wonderful barbeque under an old ground sheet strung up from the guttering and supported on two washing line props when I couldn't afford a pergola. Washing-up bowls covered in tinfoil stand in as great salad bowls and as I mentioned earlier, I once used a paint-stirrer attachment on an electric drill to mix industrial quantities of waffle batter for a charity event.

Put together a budget

Once you have thought about everything you will need and decided what you can borrow or improvise, you need to list everything along with what it will cost. If you need to hire people or buy in other services, then list that as well. This will be your budget. It may well be that you're not sure what some things will cost. If you leave a column in the list blank, you can fill in what the actual cost was when you know and keep track of how much money you have spent. Sometimes things will end up costing more than you thought. If this is the case, then you have various options: you can work out other ways to improvise to avoid some of the expenditure; obtain lower-cost items, perhaps with a reduction in quality; or you may be able to save costs elsewhere by doing more of the work yourself. There may be several trade-offs between spending time and money on something. Only you can decide what the best solution will be in order to keep to delivering your idea of success. Sometimes it can be difficult to make a decision. Keep the picture in your mind and again it will help you work out what the best course of action will be.

If all else fails, it's amazing how reliable gut instinct can be. However, failing to make any decision at all is definitely the worst possible course of action you could choose.

	Item	No	Unit	Unit cost	Total cost	Actual cost
1	French loaves	6	No.	75p	£4.50	
2	Cheese	1	kg	£10.00	£10.00	
3	Pâté	1	kg	£10.00	£10.00	
4	Butter	250	g	£1.00	£1.00	
5	Crisps	10	packs	50p	£5.00	
6	Peanuts	1	large bag	£1.50	£1.50	
7	Potatoes for baking	2	kg	£1.00	£2.00	
8	Mince	2	kg	£5.00	£10.00	
9	Tinned tomatoes	6	tins	50p	£3.00	
10	Kidney beans	6	tins	70p	£4.20	
11	Paper table cloth	2	No.	£2.00	£4.00	
12	Plastic knives & forks	2	packs	£1.00	£20.00	
13	Napkins	1	pack	£3.00	£3.00	
14	Bottles of wine	6	No	£5.00	£30.00	
15	Cartons of fruit juice	10	No.	£2.00	£20.00	
					£128.20	

Figure 6.2 Party Budget

Other people's money

There may also be ways in which you can get other money to support your project. Sometimes local businesses will sponsor certain activities for charity. In this case, you need to produce a list of companies who may help and compose an introductory letter about your project and the benefits it will bring. Think about the event from the potential sponsor's point of view – what will they gain from being involved? Can they advertise as part of the benefits? Will they get to meet potential recruits to their organisation? Could their staff gain experience?

Before you send the letter, it may well be worth contacting the organisation to identify who should receive it. Once you've written and sent the introductory letter, following it up with a phone call after a week may help ensure that it doesn't end up in the waste bin. If you feel confident, you could offer to go and talk about the benefits of sponsorship. This may seem daunting but take heart – if the company agrees to see you, then you can be reassured that you've already achieved a great deal. If they don't agree to see you, try another organisation. Make sure you're well prepared for the meeting with notes of what you want to say and keep your final picture of success in your mind. A passionate response may help to win over a reluctant sponsor.

Sharing costs

It may be possible to share some costs – perhaps by holding a joint event or by combining with someone with similar interests. Some things bought in bulk can be cheaper; my sister once bought a whole cow in order to be able to afford the meat for a fondue party. She shared the other cuts with friends and had meat in her freezer for quite some time.

Be creative

Finally, you may find some complete alternatives which will save costs. Although my husband and I did not choose to get married in the Antarctic to keep costs down, we reckon it was one of the cheapest weddings you could have, although we had wedding bells, live music and a sumptuous sit-down lunch for 12 people with lobster, fillet steak and crêpes suzette after the wedding. Always keep your mind open to alternative ways of solving a problem – you never know the benefits it may bring.

Location, location, location

There will probably be lots of other things you need for your project. You may need a specific location; for a wedding or a party that can be the critical decision – it certainly was for my wedding! It may affect a lot of other issues like the cost, the transport required (my wedding transport was a zodiac dinghy which placed severe restrictions on my wedding dress) and the timing.

Location has also affected how I trained for triathlons. It's important I get practice swimming in open water, but as I live about as far from the sea as is possible in the UK, I needed to find lakes which allow swimming. In the summer, my weekends are often focused around the open water swimming practice.

You may need to think about transport – getting to an event, or getting back home. When and where will you need the transport? You may need specialist equipment – or even knowledge to choose the right equipment. I know next to nothing about music reproduction so always need help if I am organising anything where recorded music will be played. Over the years, I have learnt a lot about what specialist equipment is needed for triathlons and have gradually accumulated items such as a heart rate monitor, a cycle computer, a power breather, a track pump and a swimming wet suit, none of which I possessed before I took up triathlons.

Limited resources need not stop you

I could not afford all of these things at once and I always managed until I could afford the next piece of equipment. If you think about your end target and prioritise what you need, whether it's time, money or anything else, you will be surprised at what can be achieved even with limited resources.

Key points

▼ *Estimate the total time your project will take*

▼ *If you don't have enough time to do everything*
- *spend less time doing other things*
- *reduce your standards*
- *get voluntary help*
- *pay for someone else to help or free up your time*

▼ *Practise estimating timescales*

▼ *Put a budget together*

▼ *You can save costs by*
- *getting sponsorship*
- *sharing costs*
- *being creative*
- *reducing standards*

▼ *Think about other resources such as*
- *location*
- *transport*
- *equipment*

CHAPTER SEVEN

You are not alone

People are the most important resource

The most important resource you have is other people. People can help you in all sorts of ways so don't let the feeling that you don't have the skills, the knowledge or any other attributes put you off tackling any big project. There is bound to be someone out there who can help.

Some people may be worried that they won't be able to trust other people, or they will lose track of what other people are doing if they enlist help. However, there are far more advantages to involving other people than disadvantages and I can't think of any major task I've undertaken that wasn't improved through involving other people.

Even individual tasks benefit from someone else's input

I've already mentioned that you may not have all the skills you need to complete a project. Any large undertaking is bound to need a variety of skills and it is no criticism if you do not have all the required skills – it would probably be some sort of superhero who did! Even something which seems to be an individual effort, like competing in a marathon or writing a book, will be much easier with other people. I've certainly found writing this book much easier when I involved other people. I used a specialist to advise me on the structure and a variety of friends and relatives to read and comment on the early drafts.

Share the load

It's not just a lack of skills that might lead you to look for people to help. It's not for nothing that there's a saying 'Many hands make light work'. Sharing the load is an important factor to think about when planning the work. It's all too easy to think we're invincible but anyone can fall ill or run into other problems. Well-run organisations realise how important this is and will ensure there is cover for when their staff go on holiday. I am a member of an engineering organisation and one of the local area committees had a great idea and ensured that each person who volunteered to organise an event had a 'buddy' so that if the person organising had a problem or needed help, there would be someone ready at hand. The idea has been adopted by all the other areas – there's always someone to carry on if one person has a problem. It also means that the two people learn from each other.

Off days

We also all have 'off days' and it's useful to have someone to support you through them. It can be all too easy to think we have to be super man or woman in order to tackle a major task but that's not necessary with the help of people who can cover for you or fill in those skills or traits you don't happen to possess.

A different view point

It can be very useful to have someone who can provide a different viewpoint. They may think of things you have not thought of – another well-known saying is 'Two heads are better than one'. In my case, as someone who is sometimes apt to forget things, having someone who can check for any lapses in my memory is really helpful. These days, it tends to be my husband who knows I have a tendency to forget things and will keep an eye on my diary to make sure I don't forget important dates and remind me to take things with me which he knows I have forgotten before – like keys, tickets, diary, purse and my laptop – yes, I really am that scatterbrained!

Different characters

It can also be useful to include people who have different character traits from you. If you are an optimist, it can be very useful to have someone who is rather more pessimistic who might flag up problems which you had not thought of. Similarly, if you are an introvert who finds dealing with people difficult, then it could be useful to rope in someone who is much more comfortable dealing with people. Some people have lots of ideas but may not be very good at following things through until they are finished. Other people are hopeless at thinking about detail but are really good at seeing the big picture. If they work on their own, they risk missing important actions or may do some tasks badly as it just does not interest them.

One Minute Millionaire team

The need to allow for differences in character has been identified as an important factor by a number of experts who have studied how teams work. Mark Victor Hansen, who wrote a book 'One Minute Millionaire', suggested it's useful to have four different types in any team. These four people he called hare, owl, squirrel and turtle. The hare is the ideas person, the owl is good at creating action plans, the squirrel is the detail person and the turtle is the person who identifies the problems. These four types all have a role to play and it can be very important to make sure that each of these roles is not neglected.

Don't be afraid of your opposites

One person I know is a born optimist and started her own business. She put together a business plan which looked very favourable. However, she ran into all sorts of problems, some of which might have been spotted if she'd involved someone as the turtle character. The problem was she doesn't like negative people and so didn't talk to the people who might have provided some constructive criticism. Sometimes the different character traits may make someone difficult to get on with, but try to recognise the benefit of their difference and work with it.

Personally, I'm not very good at detail so squirrels are always welcome in my team as that way I make sure that all the little things which can make the difference between something being 'OK' and something being 'superb' are not overlooked. However, I get impatient with that level of detail. Over the years, I've learnt to bite my lip if a 'squirrel' picks up problems which I think are unimportant – they could make the difference between success and failure.

Belbin's teams

Another author, Belbin, suggested that eight different types are needed in any team. These covered detail and overview roles, people who start things and people who would finish things off, people who liked to work on their own and people who are better working alongside others. You may not need eight different people, but it is useful to think about what your own strengths and weaknesses are and where it would be useful to have people to complement your character traits as well as filling gaps in your practical skills. Sometimes it can be hard to identify your own character traits, but your family or close friends might be prepared to say what your strengths and weaknesses are. I've listed some key areas to think about:

▼ *Are you gregarious and like working with other people or do you prefer being on your own?*

▼ *Are you a 'detail' person or do you prefer to think about the big picture?*

▼ *Are you an optimist or a pessimist?*

▼ *Do you like starting things but aren't so good at finishing things off?*

▼ *Do you like to follow logical steps or do you jump around with your ideas?*

▼ *Do you have loads of energy or do you flag easily?*

▼ *Do you like being in charge or do you prefer to be just part of the team?*

▼ *Do you like the limelight or shrink back if everyone is looking at you?*

If you remember, in Chapter 4 I described Edward de Bono's 'Six Thinking Hats' and you may be able to get some clues by thinking which 'hat' comes most easily to you and which ones feel more unnatural. For example, if you find the creative approach – the green hat – more difficult, try to find someone with creative flair to provide that side to your plans.

Don't always go for the comfortable option

So who should you involve in any project? It may not necessarily be someone you feel comfortable with. Like the optimist I mentioned earlier, you may find that people with traits opposite to yours are not easy to get along with. However, if you recognise that their character is filling a gap and serving a purpose, you may be able to get on with them better and even learn from them.

Missing skills

Apart from character traits, you also need to think about the skills needed which you don't have. What gaps need filling? You may not be any good at public speaking and need someone to give a vote of thanks. You may need someone who is comfortable with computers whereas you are not.

You may remember that some of the negative aspects I identified when using the Six Thinking Hats approach on my house extension were that I needed someone to draw up the plans, help me with the planning and to do the building. By asking around, I was able to find a very good building technician and, with his help, I obtained planning permission. Other friends recommended builders – or told me of their friends and neighbours who had had good quality building work done, so I ended up with a reasonable list of builders to ask to quote.

Avoid the things you don't enjoy

Another reason why you may want to include people is that you may not like doing all of the work required; even if you really want to finish the project, there may be parts you don't enjoy at all. It's OK not to enjoy doing some things; some people hate tidying up, others love it. If you're organising a big event and don't want to be left with the clearing up, try to find people who don't mind staying on at the end or coming in early the next day to do it. I hate proofreading things and I can assure you that I have not proofread this book myself. However, my husband doesn't mind doing it and is very good at spotting mistakes. Guess who I'll get to do this book!

Cast the net wide

When you're thinking about who to involve, it's important to cast the net wide. For a start, most people have a limited number of friends and family who can feel put upon if they keep being asked for help. If they see that you've asked a range of other people, it may actually encourage them to assist.

Seven Degrees of Separation

Even if you don't know someone with the right skills or qualities, don't worry. There is a theory called 'The Seven Degrees of Separation'. This is the idea that you can find a connection to anyone on earth through just six other people, i.e. there are just seven steps between you and whoever you need. You know someone who knows someone else who knows someone else and so on, until the last person knows the targeted person. In this way, we should be able to find a connection to Prince Charles, Angelina Jolie or David Beckham.

If someone can't help, ask them for a suggestion for someone who can

Of course, you may not need to find quite such specific people. Perhaps you want someone who can do flower arrangements, write press releases or install a new programme on your computer. If you ask everyone you know, even if they can't help, ask them to give you ideas about who could help you to find the right person. Then go to the person suggested and ask if they can help, with an alternative contact if they can't help directly. It's a bit like the treasure hunts where a clue sends you somewhere else and you find a clue there which sends you to the next place and so on.

Networking

These days that sort of contact is called networking. A modern version of this is the electronic network, such as LinkedIn or Facebook, which is also worth investigating. However it's really just a matter of asking people; if they can't help you themselves, can they suggest someone who can, whether you do that face to face, via the telephone or over the internet. The good thing is that as you approach different people, you widen your circle of contacts and may find all sorts of other sources of help on the way.

I recently started breeding alpacas with my husband. This was something totally new to me; I had always considered myself 'a bit of a townie' and even my husband who had lived in the country for some time had never bred livestock. However, by asking around we started meeting people who could help – other breeders who lived quite close, vets who could advise and local suppliers who tracked down the specialist food and equipment we needed. We joined the British Alpaca Society and went to their local events, meeting even more people who could help as well as learning from the events themselves.

Of course, it may not always be easy getting people to help. However, there's lots of advice on how to work with other people in Chapter 8.

Talk to people

It's important you don't just think about the people who will help you with doing some of the work. There may be other people involved in the project that you need to think about. In some cases they just need to be aware of what's happening. Maybe you need to talk to them because they'd be hurt if you didn't or because if they found out from anyone but you, they could be really awkward. Often relatives come into this category. They may wonder why you've decided to embark upon something or bring up some embarrassing event from your past: the time when you tried to organise a party when you were ten and no-one came; or the time you came last in the egg and spoon race at the school sports. Think about when to talk to these sorts of people – perhaps having a small success under your belt might give you confidence before you tackle them, but think about the consequences of leaving things until later. Hearing something about someone close to you from a third party can be hurtful.

Maybe you need to involve them because they'll be really supportive. Never under-estimate the value of someone at the end of a phone who can just say 'Well done' for each small step forward or 'Never mind' when you've had a setback. They can be worth their weight in gold. These days with email you can rope in support from all sorts of directions.

Who might de-rail a project?

Finally you may need to think about people you should involve because if you don't, they could get in the way, or block your progress. In some cases they could be members of your family or close friends. A spouse or child may feel threatened if you decide to take on a major challenge. They may wonder if, with all the time you'll be spending on your new project, you will have any time for them. They may wonder if it will change you.

Work out ways in which you can get them on your side, or how you can carry on working even if they are not supportive.

Keep people informed

Outside of your immediate circle, you need to think if there are other people to be involved. Should neighbours be aware? Does your local council need to be informed? Often a carefully-worded approach early on, in a low-key fashion, will pay dividends later.

If you're planning something which may get a mixed response or which could be controversial, it can be useful to sit down and draw up a list of supporters, objectors and neutral people. You might make it part of your action plan then to talk to the supporters to ask for their help in overcoming the objections, or to work on the neutral people to get them to be more supportive. You may need to think about who your greatest opponents might be and then think about how you can minimise their opposition. List what you think might be their reasons for objecting and then come up with a counter-argument against each reason. If you speak to people face to face and involve them as early as possible, that can often help defuse their opposition. Making sure that you've dealt with potential opposition and 'blockers' is one of the secrets of success for any project.

I recently received a very considerately-worded letter from a neighbour explaining that, as part of their wedding celebrations, they would be having a clay pigeon shoot and some fireworks. They apologised for the noise in advance and invited everyone in my house to join in their celebrations if we were free that day. It was only a short letter but worked perfectly because, as far as I was concerned, I understood why there might be some noise and would be far more tolerant than if they had not warned me.

Any major task will need some input from other people, even if it's only support and understanding from your friends and family. Making the best use of other people's contribution can make a huge difference to your chances of success. There really is truth in the saying 'Many hands make light work'.

Key Points

▼ *The most important resource you have is other people*

▼ *Other people can*
- *share the load*
- *get you through off days*
- *provide a different point of view*
- *bring different skills*

▼ *It can be useful to have different characters in a team*
- *some of the most difficult people to get on with may be the most useful*

▼ *If you don't have a contact yourself, ask around*

▼ *Make sure all the important people know what you are doing*

▼ *Think about who might de-rail your project and work out ways to prevent it*

CHAPTER EIGHT

Getting people to do things

People are generally willing to help

We've looked at why you need to involve other people and how they can help – or even hinder. Still, working with other people is not always easy, particularly if you're not used to it. The good news, however, is that the majority of people are generally willing to help from the outset and in virtually all the projects and challenges I've undertaken, I've been amazed at how kind and helpful people have been. If you approach people positively, I'm sure you'll find plenty of helpful people out there.

Look at things from other people's point of view

It may help to get people on your side if you think about what will motivate them. Getting them to help may require you to think about things from their point of view. There is an old American Indian saying 'You must walk a mile in another man's shoes to understand them'. Whilst you can't put yourself in everyone else's place, it is important that you try to see things from their point of view. What might motivate a teenage lad to help is likely to be rather different from a busy mother of three or a retired widower. You might need to think about what things they seem to like, which may not be what you like yourself.

The people who helped me with my triathlon generally did it because they enjoyed seeing people get fitter and improve. As that was the case, it was important that I gave them feedback so that they could have the pleasure of knowing that I was following their advice and gaining from it.

In some cases, you may need to explain how their participation will benefit them. For instance, if you are doing something for your own community then explaining to individuals how that will particularly help them may persuade them to give up time.

How will people benefit?

You may get young people to participate if you explain that their input could be put on their CV to help them get a good job or a good place at college. A concert hall near where I live is run almost entirely by volunteers, including all the technical roles required for the sound and lighting, and young people relish the opportunity to gain experience which could help them find a professional role later on. Some people work there to get a chance to see bands and musicians for free, whilst others do it as they enjoy meeting the other volunteers and the social life that it gives them. The important thing is that they all feel they gain something from working there.

Tell people why you think they can help

If you ask some people to help, they may wonder why you asked them in particular and if they have special skills or characteristics, they may be very pleased if you explain this to them. Perhaps you value their attention to detail or their stamina. Make sure you tell them – it may help sway them to be part of your team.

Counter their arguments

If you think they might say no to your request, then think about why that might be and see if you can come up with a counter-argument. Try writing down why they might not help and then come up with a counter-argument. Think of how this could be a win/win situation – what might they gain from working with you? For example, if they helped you prepare for your party, could you return the favour later with some event of theirs? Is there any other assistance you can offer them? There might also be a lesser role they could play. If you've asked for something and they say they can't help, they may then agree to something which is not so onerous if you put that to them subsequently.

You can still ask for contacts

Remind yourself that the worst thing that can happen is that they will say they won't help. You can then at least ask them if they can suggest anyone else who might be able to assist. If you're really worried about asking people directly, you can try the approach of asking initially if they can suggest someone who can help. You may be pleasantly surprised and find they offer themselves, but at worst you may have another contact to ask. Whatever their response, don't forget to thank them – you never know if you might need to approach them again in the future. Whatever you do, don't put off asking people, however daunting you may find it. The more notice you give them, the easier it will be for them to help and if the worst should happen and they can't help, then you've more time to ask other people.

Share your vision

Another powerful way to get people to support your venture is to share your vision with them. Explain why you want to undertake this project and tell them about the picture you have developed. You could think about what success might mean to other people so you may be able to tell them how a successful project will benefit them. Bring in all the senses as I explained before so that they can see and feel the picture. Enthusiasm is infectious, so use your enthusiasm for the project to persuade other people.

Have a go

Generally, I have found that if you approach people in a positive frame of mind, they respond well and it may restore your faith in mankind. Often people are better at putting across their ideas than they think they are, so just have a go and see what happens. The worst that will happen is that they say no, in which case you are no worse off than you were. Don't forget in this case to ask if they have a suggestion as to someone else who might help.

Explain what you expect

Once you've enlisted some help then it's important that you channel their enthusiasm and direct their input. The first thing you must do is make sure that any helpers know what you expect. You will need to be very clear about what you want them to do. A written note can be helpful, even for quite an informal arrangement, and email is great for this as it doesn't seem quite as formal as a letter but gives you a chance to list exactly what you need. Make sure they understand your picture for success and listen to what they want to get out of helping, so that you can try to ensure their needs are met too.

Get everyone together

Once you've sorted out who is doing what, if you're using quite a lot of helpers it can be useful to get everyone together early on. This can be a very informal meeting or even a social event – coffee and cakes at someone's house or drinks at the local pub. This gives everyone a chance to learn what part each person is playing in your overall plan and to sort out who they need to talk to. It can save you having to tell several people the same thing over again and allow everyone to hear answers to questions that maybe they didn't think of but are actually quite helpful. It may prevent duplication or may even identify some gaps that you hadn't spotted.

How teams behave

Once the members of your team of helpers have met, don't worry too much if everything does not go smoothly initially. Teams need to get to know each other and I have heard the stages they go through described as 'form, storm, norm, perform'. This means that in a team there may be disagreements initially until everyone has sorted out what their role is and how to get along together. However, once they sort that out and have established the 'norm' with a basis to work on, they then go from strength to strength and get better and better. So don't worry if you see some conflict early on, it may well be part of the 'storm' which the team need to go through to perform. However, make sure you watch how people interact. A soothing word or some encouragement can work wonders to nip problems in the bud, and the ability of everyone to get on together can make a real difference to the success or otherwise of a project.

Problem people

You will find that some people are easier to work with than others and you may encounter some common problems. For instance, the person who promises whatever you ask but never delivers. The best way to find them out is to make sure you check on their progress well before they need to be finished. If you have any concerns, it could be as well to have a back-up plan. A friend of mine frequently offers to help but never delivers. I now know what to expect and I check regularly whether something is being done and sometimes have alternative plans if it seems she will not finish what she agreed to do.

Negativity

Some people can be very negative and only seem to find the problems. If you listen to their grumbles and predictions you may find that they start to pull your mood down as well and, in the worst case, your confidence could take a knocking. There are several ways you can tackle this problem. One is to limit your contact with them, which works if you know they will get on with something in spite of their complaints. Another is to talk to them directly about the effect they are having with their negativity. It is possible that they haven't realised how they come across. It may be possible to use that negativity to identify things which may go wrong and how to be ready for them. If they suggest a potential problem, throw it back at them and ask them how they would overcome it. If they find that their concerns are being listened to and taken account of, it may reduce their complaining. However, some people are just born negative, so accept it if they won't change and see if you can make use of the trait as a positive benefit.

Minimum effort

Some people do what's required but with the minimum of effort so that the result is not what you had expected or hoped. Not everyone may have your level of motivation to deliver the best possible contribution and their assistance may sometimes be a little grudging. This can be a particular problem if you enlist the help of your family. The best way to make sure this doesn't happen is to write down exactly what you want. Specify exactly what the outputs should be like. For instance, if you want a poster with pictures that is eye-catching, say that, rather than just asking for a poster. If you want live professional entertainment rather than a few CDs playing in the background, again, make it clear.

Talkers

A common problem is people who never stop talking so that things don't get done. You will need to be tough with them. If you find it hard to interrupt their stream of chatter, say their name firmly and repeat it several times until you break their flow. You can then either allow someone else to speak or you can point out by when the work needs to be completed and suggest that time is marching on.

Tactless

There are also those sorts of people who seem to upset everyone else and always seem to say the wrong thing. An easy way to deal with these people is to find something for them to do which allows them to work on their own. If they do need to work with other people, you may have to warn the others or ensure you are present to act as peacemaker.

Look for people's strengths

If you are working with volunteers you don't always have the option as to who you have to help, but even at work you cannot always choose your colleagues so you can find the same problems there as well. However, if you look for people's strengths and try to minimise the impact of their weaknesses, then you will find you can get positive input from everyone. Try to use their different strengths to complement your skills and character.

Paid help

Of course, if you can pay someone to help that may resolve some problems. We can sometimes be wary of paying someone we know, but this can make a huge difference. When I was working on my MBA I ended up with only a few weeks to complete my dissertation before I left to work in Afghanistan. I could not get other people to write my dissertation, but a friend of mine was a professional editor and I paid her to go through it and edit it, which saved some time and ensured I finished the report before I left. Naturally, I checked this was not against the college rules before I did it!

Read the contract

If you are employing someone, you still need to make sure that they understand exactly what to do. In some cases you may need to sign a formal contract – for instance when hiring caterers, entertainers or a vehicle. This may seem a boring task but it really is important that you read the small print. You need to know what your commitment will be if you have to cancel. You may want to be assured of what staffing or equipment will be provided or how they will ensure that the quality is what you expect; exactly when they expect to be paid, and in what form of payment also needs to be made clear. Musicians often expect to be paid at the end of their session, which may not be the end of the event. Therefore, you need to make sure that you've brought a cheque book or the cash with you. If there is no formal contract, a letter listing everything that you expect them to do is important and well worth the time and effort, even if you know them well. Any special requirements can be included such as maximum volumes for a band or disco, where people can park for loading and unloading, or what access they will have prior to the event to prepare or to clear up afterwards.

Praise work well done

An important factor to remember when anyone is helping you, whether paid or as a volunteer, and whether friends, family, neighbours, colleagues or contractors, is that people respond well to positive feedback. Don't wait until the end if there's something which is going well before then. A positive word may well ensure that someone keeps motivated through to the end. It will reassure them that they are doing things as you want. If you are using children as helpers this is especially important, but it does work with adults too!

You may not see yourself as a manager but if you have people who are helping you with any project then you will need to use some management skills. There is nothing mysterious about these skills – the key is to treat people as you would like to be treated yourself but remember that different people are motivated by different things. This chapter has suggested some of those skills, which will help ensure that you get the best out of your team, whoever they are and whatever they are doing. It will also help to ensure that if you're using friends and family to help, they're still friends with you when the project is finished and won't mind helping you again in the future.

Key points

▼ *People are generally willing to help*

▼ *Think about things from their point of view*

▼ *If people can't or won't help you, ask them to suggest someone who will*

▼ *Ensure you clarify exactly what you want from them*

▼ *Work on building your team*

    - get everyone together if you can

    - accept that some teams don't always work at first

    - develop strategies for difficult people

▼ *Praise work well done*

CHAPTER NINE

Make sure things happen

Organise your information

So far you've put a lot of thought into how and what you need to organise. This planning is important and will pay dividends. You may not have the luxury of doing all your planning at one time or in one place and you need to collect everything together you have worked on so far. Compile it all into a folder. Sort it into clear sections – keep one section for anything you've prepared regarding your end picture (your definition of success) and put everything to do with costs in another section, perhaps with a summary budget at the front. You could put all your thoughts about people who can help, whether you've asked them, whether they've said yes, in another section and the action plan in another section. Prepare lists for equipment, guests, food and anything else so that it will make it easy to check progress.

Keep your goals visible

Make everything as easy as possible to refer to. Keep the file with all the information somewhere you can get to easily to check or update things. It's also a good idea to have some sort of picture of your end goal somewhere you can see it regularly. This will help keep you motivated, to continue to remind you why you are doing the various activities and even making some sacrifices such as getting up early in the morning or foregoing watching Coronation Street in the evening. It will make sure you have a clear picture in your mind so that when you have decisions to make you will know exactly what you want, which will help you choose the path you should opt for.

Keep the action plan visible

It's also helpful if you keep the action plan readily visible. This might be the original piece of paper with the post-its arranged, or it could be a smaller plan you've prepared based on the post-its. A simple way to keep track of your progress is to make a list of the actions with four columns. Two of these columns are the planned start and finish date. Leave the other two columns blank so that you can write down the actual start and finish dates against the plan. You can see an example of this in Figure 5.7.

Bar charts

If you like pictures, a good way of showing what you have to do and when is to list the activities down the right hand side of the page with dates along the top, at daily, weekly or monthly intervals. For each activity, show a line starting at the earliest time you could start it and stretching until you must finish the activity in order to complete everything in time. This is called a bar chart and is easy to draw out or prepare on a computer using a spreadsheet programme like Excel. If you leave space below each line, you can show the actual timing of each action below what you planned, which makes it easy to keep track of everything. Two examples of bar charts are shown in Figures 9.2 and 9.3. One of them has been drawn in Excel and the other has been drawn by hand.

Draw charts on a computer

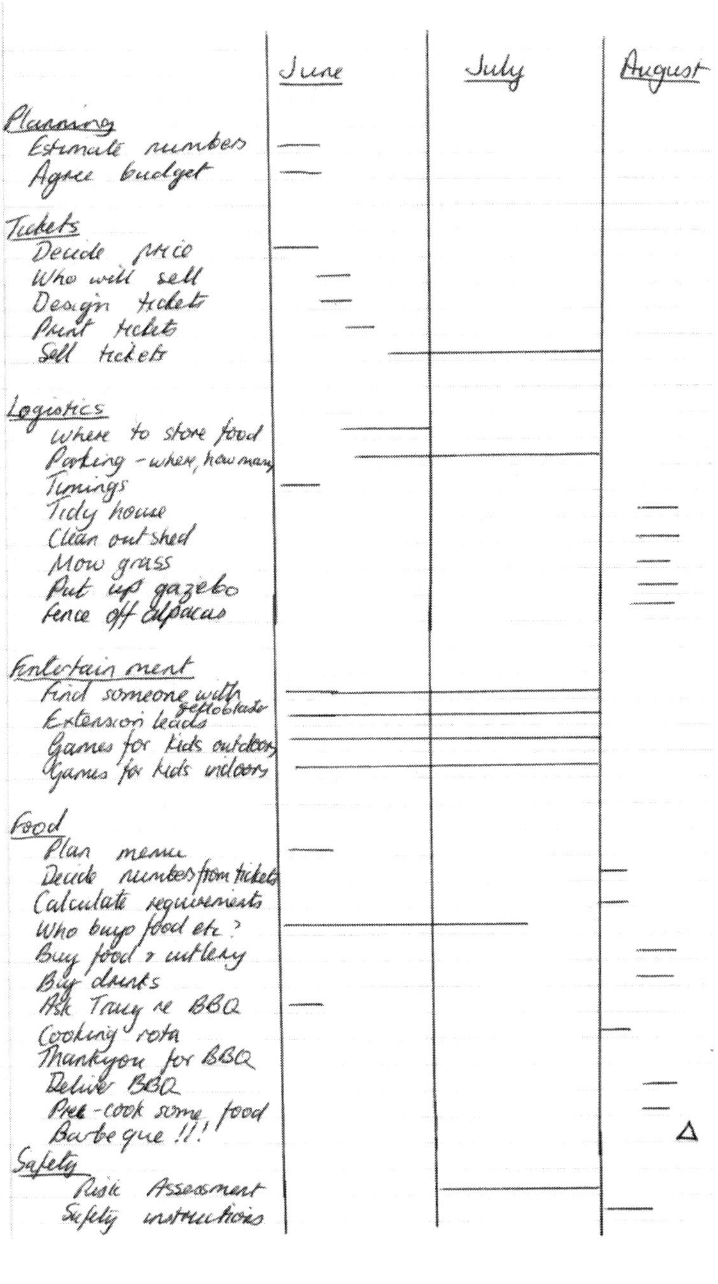

Figure 9.2 Bar chart drawn by hand

	June				July				August			
	7	14	21	28	5	12	19	26	2	9	16	23
Planning												
Estimate numbers	▓											
Agree budget	▓											
Tickets												
Decide price	▓											
Decide who sells		▓	▓									
Design tickets		▓	▓									
Print tickets				▓								
Sell tickets					▓	▓	▓	▓	▓	▓		
Logistics												
Where to store food		▓	▓	▓								
Parking arrangements		▓	▓	▓	▓	▓	▓	▓	▓	▓		
Timings	▓											
Tidy house										▓	▓	
Clean out shed										▓	▓	
Mow grass												▓
Put up gazebo												▓
Fence off alpacas												

	June				July				August			
	7	14	21	28	5	12	19	26	2	9	16	23
Entertainment												
Borrow ghetto blaster	▓	▓	▓	▓	▓	▓	▓	▓	▓	▓	▓	
Extension leads	▓	▓	▓	▓	▓	▓	▓	▓	▓	▓	▓	
Games for kids outdoors	▓	▓	▓	▓	▓	▓	▓	▓	▓	▓	▓	
Games for kids indoors	▓	▓	▓	▓	▓	▓	▓	▓	▓	▓	▓	
Food												
Plan menu	▓	▓	▓									
Decide numbers from tickets											▓	
Calculate requirements											▓	
Decide who buys what	▓	▓	▓	▓	▓	▓	▓	▓	▓			
Buy food & cutlery											▓	
Buy drinks											▓	
Borrow BBQ	▓	▓	▓	▓	▓	▓	▓					
Cooking rota											▓	
Thank you for BBQ												▓
Pre-cook food												▓
BBQ												█

Figure 9.3 Bar chart drawn in Excel

Cross off your actions

You are now ready to start carrying out your actions. In Chapter 4, I talked about how to overcome the problem of getting started if you are finding that difficult. Once you are under way with your action plan, it's important to keep track of how you are progressing. As you start each activity, make a note on your action plan of when you actually started. If you have the action plan displayed somewhere you can see it, this makes a wonderful picture of how you are progressing, and it can be really satisfying to see the actions marked off one by one. If you still have the original post-its up, you can draw a big cross over each one in felt tip as you complete it. Making a note of the date you finished it on the post-it will also help you to track progress. If you have drawn up a bar chart as I showed in Figure 9.4 then mark the actions in another colour or shading. For actions which take a long time, such as completing part of a study course, you may want to shade off sections of the bar as you do more and more.

In the barbeque example in Figure 9.4 all the preliminary decisions such as estimated numbers, ticket price, budget and menu have been completed by mid-June. Someone had volunteered to lend us a proper professional-standard barbeque and I'd cleared out an old deep-freezer which we could use to store the food. However, we hadn't managed to get anyone to agree to sell the tickets and collect the money. However, that wasn't a problem just yet as that still left over a month to sell tickets. However, it's easy to see that if we don't find a ticket seller it will reduce the time available to sell tickets.

Keep track of your progress

	June				July				August			
	7	14	21	28	5	12	19	26	2	9	16	23
Planning												
Estimate numbers	▓											
Agree budget	▓											
Tickets												
Decide price	▓											
Decide who sells		▓	▓									
Design tickets		▓	▓									
Print tickets				▓								
Sell tickets					▓	▓	▓	▓	▓			
Logistics												
Where to store food		▓	▓	▓								
Parking arrangements		▓	▓	▓	▓	▓	▓	▓	▓			
Timings	▓											
Tidy house										▓	▓	
Clean out shed										▓	▓	
Mow grass												▓
Put up gazebo												▓
Fence off alpacas												

Continued over page

	June				July				August			
	7	14	21	28	5	12	19	26	2	9	16	23
Entertainment												
Borrow ghetto blaster	■	■	■	■	■	■	■	■	■	■	■	
Extension leads	■	■	■	■	■	■	■	■	■	■	■	
Games for kids outdoors	■	■	■	■	■	■	■	■	■	■	■	
Games for kids indoors	■	■	■	■	■	■	■	■	■	■	■	
Food												
Plan menu	■	■	■									
Decide numbers from tickets											■	
Calculate requirements											■	
Decide who buys what	■	■	■	■	■	■	■	■	■			
Buy food & cutlery											■	
Buy drinks											■	
Borrow BBQ	■	■	■	■	■	■	■	■	■	■	■	
Cooking rota											■	
Thank you for BBQ												■
Pre-cook food												■
BBQ												■

Figure 9.4 Bar chart with activities marked off

It's useful to keep a notebook with you all the time to record any actions, phone calls or ideas that might come to you. You never know when these may come along. If you develop the habit of writing everything down, then that will be a valuable record of when things happened or what was agreed. I developed the habit when I was working on site. I never knew when the contractor would speak to me and we might agree something. If I made a note there and then in a notebook small enough to keep in my pocket, it paid dividends and, in fact, was invaluable on one construction project when a gas bottle leak lead to an explosion in my site office such that all my papers were spread all over the construction site. My little notebook was at home with me and was vital in sorting out what I'd agreed with the contractor. I hope you don't suffer such a catastrophe but it does show how small actions can protect you from disaster. I also find it incredibly useful as I don't have the world's best memory and keeping a note of things helps make sure I don't forget them.

Keep your folder up to date

If possible, transfer information from your notebook to the project folder. Each time you spend anything on the project, record what you've spent on the list. If it varies from your original estimate then check how that will affect the final total of expenditure. If you find that lots of costs are higher than you budgeted for, then the earlier you find that out the easier it will be to sort out some alternative action. This may allow you to keep within your budget or to work out how you get some extra funds.

It's also useful to keep a note of any agreements – whether these are informal such as someone agreeing to help with something, or formal like copies of contracts for the hire of musicians, catering or accommodation. Keep copies of anything you send out in your file if you've done them as 'hard' copies.

Filing on a computer

If you are using a computer for much of this work, make sure you set up a folder on the system specifically for this project. Within that you can set up sub-folders; for example financial items with perhaps a budget spreadsheet. You can have folders for copies of letters or emails. It can sometimes take a lot of self-discipline to make sure everything is filed away properly but it really does help to keep track of things.

A chronological diary can be helpful and I also keep a hard-cover notebook by my phone in which I make a note of what transpired from any phone calls I make or receive at home. That's proved a huge benefit and has done away with the myriad of notes and scraps of papers which can always be mislaid or destroyed.

Use your filed information

Keeping a record of everything is important but will not help you if you don't use the information. You need to review the action plan and your budget regularly to make sure that everything is on track. Don't forget to monitor any actions which other people are carrying out for you – whether they are being paid to do the work or are giving their time for free.

Managing other people's deadlines

Do not rely on other people to always meet the deadlines they agree to. They may not intend to miss them but other people have different priorities, so you will need to encourage them to keep on track. If they seem to be falling behind with something they volunteered to do, then you will need to tackle this with tact and diplomacy. Ask them whether they are sure they will finish on time. If they offer you assurances, then point out why you have concerns and ask how they will make up time or speed up their activity. It is always helpful to work out some alternative options before you talk to them, such as suggestions of who might be able to help or a proposal to reduce the amount of work they do. However, try to avoid making people lose face and always keep in mind that you might want their help again.

Your action may be guided by past experience. If they have failed to deliver in the past then you may have an alternative plan right from the start. Earlier I mentioned a friend who is rather unreliable. However sometimes I do not like to leave her out of my plans. In that case I usually have someone else lined up to work alongside of her and I check what she is doing early on.

Use milestones

The milestones you decided on in your action plan are particularly helpful here as it makes it easy to see how you are progressing and, if you are behind in your programme, by how much. However, you don't have to wait for a milestone to check progress. If you have a task which is spread over some time, work out how long it will take in total and then check when you are around half or a quarter of the way through to see if it is taking the time you thought. Again, it's much better to identify that things are taking longer as early as possible. Keeping your records easy to access will make this much easier and if the action plan is up on the wall, you can see at a glance how you are doing.

Making up time

If things are taking less time then there's generally no reason to worry, although if it relates to something done by someone else it might be a good idea to check the quality of what they are doing, if that's appropriate. If you find that things are taking longer than you thought, you may need to take action. However, first of all think about whether this will affect the overall outcome. Will it mean that you finish the whole project late? Do you have any spare time which means that running late with this particular activity does not really matter? I must admit that I tend to be rather over-optimistic with how long things will take. Whilst I have learnt to allow spare time to take my optimism into account, it has meant that, for instance, I have had to work very late into the night, rearrange social events or get up early in order to get things done. However, I have a good record of delivering, both in my work and in my private life.

What to do if you're behind the plan

If running late will affect the timing of the whole project, then you have a similar range of options open to you as you had when you were preparing the action plan originally. You could change the overall timing of the project, get extra help, pay other people to help, find more time or accept a lower quality output. Have a look at Chapter 6 again to remind you of these options. However, you will need to do something and the sooner you decide exactly what, the better.

When I was training for my first triathlon, I had set myself a target of being able to swim 400 metres front crawl without stopping a month before my first race. As it turned out, I just could not manage this. However, I could swim 400 metres without stopping if I alternated front crawl and breaststroke. I changed to that approach and swam my first race with a mix of the two strokes. It did mean that my legs worked harder during the swim phase than they would have done if I'd just swum crawl, but I still achieved my overall targets of completing the race, having fun and not being last, so as far as I was concerned it was a success.

In the barbeque example I used earlier, I had difficulties finding a ticket seller. As the deadline I had set for finding someone got closer, I went ahead and printed the tickets and sent a notice to everyone without the ticket seller details on it so that people put the date in their diaries. I did eventually persuade someone to sell the tickets and, when that was agreed, I sent an email to everyone saying how they could buy tickets, which also acted as a reminder about the event.

Check the budget

In a similar way, you need to check the budget regularly. If you enter costs as they occur as I described earlier in this chapter, it should not be difficult to track. Once again, the earlier you spot a problem, the easier it will be to work out how to overcome it and you could employ any of the ideas in Chapter 6 to work out how to reduce the remaining costs to get back to budget. Alternatively, you might accept that things will cost more. If the project involves producing a lot of smaller items for a specific cost, then checking the unit costs can be helpful. Suppose you're cooking batches of sweets for sale at a market. Check the total cost when you have cooked a few batches of sweets to make sure that they are costing what you originally estimated. Early checks like this can make all the difference and ensure that you don't overstretch yourself.

Investigate any variations

If the costs aren't going to plan, it's useful to think in a little more detail what has caused the difference. Were you too optimistic originally? Have prices increased since you drew up your original plan? This may help you to review the remaining costs in your budget and, if necessary, revise these as well. When I set up my engineering business, I found that the cost of buying my computer, printer, fax, etc. was rather more than I expected, so I cut back on buying stationery and publicity to keep within what I could afford. As it turned out, I had plenty of work and four years on I still haven't prepared a publicity leaflet as all my work comes from recommendations. It's surprising how it's possible to cut back on costs and still achieve your original goals.

Plan, do, review and revise

Your plan is there to help and to show early on if there may be a problem; however, it is not written in tablets of stone. If you keep going back to the plan and revising it as you learn about costs and timings, then it will get more and more realistic and your skills at predicting these things will also improve. Keep going through a cycle of 'plan, do, review and revise' and you will keep on track.

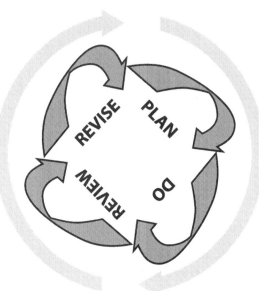

Figure 9.5 Plan Do Review Revise

Key points

▼ *Keep all your information readily to hand*

▼ *Try to keep a picture of your goal somewhere visible*

▼ *Develop a bar chart to track your progress*

▼ *Ensure you update your plan regularly*

▼ *Check other people's deadlines in good time*

▼ *Identify if you're behind time or over your budget as soon as possible and take action if required*

▼ *Plan, Do, Review, Revise*

You can make your own luck

Make your own luck

There will probably be some of those amongst you who have been saying from early on 'It's all very well to plan but nothing ever goes according to plan, so why bother?' Whilst it's true that things do not always go as we planned, it's possible to be ready for these eventualities so that if they occur you can change your plans and still arrive at your goal successfully. Some people appear to be very lucky, but often this is because they make their own luck. In this chapter, I'll show that you have more control than you think and that you, too, can make your own luck.

Bring out the black hat

All sorts of things can go wrong with any venture. The trick is to think about these things in advance so that you come up with ways to reduce the likelihood of the risk happening, or to reduce the impact of the risk if it cannot be avoided. If you go back to Edward de Bono's six hats in Chapter 7, this is the time when you wear the black hat. This is also the time when any 'turtle-type' friends will come in useful, using the types of people that Mark Victor Hansen suggests you need in a team, also described in Chapter 7. This is especially true if you are an eternal optimist and find taking off the rose-tinted spectacles quite difficult.

Think of everything that could go wrong

What you need to do is think of everything that could possibly go wrong. The brain-storming technique I described in Chapter 4 works well here. Make sure you have invited your most pessimistic friends or members of the family and ensure they understand that you give them full licence to think of absolutely everything that could go wrong. Pass round the everyday object for which people have to think of new uses, and then get everyone writing down the problems which could occur.

Suppose you're planning a party. You might come up with a list of problems something like this one below.

▼ *Not many people can come*
▼ *Booze runs out early*
▼ *Uncle Fred gets drunk and does a striptease*
▼ *Someone loses their coat/bag and gets upset*
▼ *Someone drops red wine on my best rug*
▼ *I over-order on the French bread and am eating stale bread for a week*
▼ *My two sisters have an argument and everyone else is embarrassed*
▼ *People don't like the music*
▼ *My CD player packs up*
▼ *People don't like the food*
▼ *Nobody talks to each other*
▼ *My glasses/crockery/furniture gets broken*
▼ *The neighbours complain of the noise*
▼ *The neighbours complain about the parking*

Rank all the problems

Now there are quite a lot of things that could go wrong and you may not have time to think of solutions to all of them, so it's useful to rank them. You do this by giving each problem two different marks.

First work out how likely something is to happen. This does not have to be an absolute; just decide whether something is highly likely to happen, a possibility or quite unlikely.

For instance, you may have very difficult neighbours and can almost guarantee that they'll complain about the noise. However, there's a reasonable amount of space in the road so the possibility of them complaining about the parking is less likely, but still possible, so that's a medium risk. All your friends are party animals and the chances of not many people coming is very unlikely, but your two sisters really do not get on well so you may put that as fairly likely again. You may think it inevitable that something will get broken, but generally again your friends and relatives are a pretty gregarious lot (especially after a few drinks) so the chances of them not talking are low.

The consequences

Now think about the consequences of each problem occurring. You may have a fairly old set of glasses and crockery and your furniture may be mainly cheap and cheerful, so the consequences of something getting broken might not be too serious. Of course, if you only have crystal glasses and Royal Doulton china, it's a different matter. You might feel that running out of booze early would severely affect your future standing with your friends, so you'd consider that serious, whilst if your sisters argue, it's not the first time and everyone else will ignore it, although you would be embarrassed at the time, so that's a medium consequence.

You might feel that a party is not a party without everyone up and dancing so people not liking the music and the CD packing up would be really serious. So could the neighbours complaining about the noise, as they are just the sort to call the police, but they're less likely to do that if someone's parked across their drive – they'd just knock on your door, so that's only a medium consequence. Against each problem, mark either 1, 2 or 3 according to whether the likelihood of the problem occurring is low, medium or high. Then mark in a second column a 1, 2 or 3 according to the seriousness of the results from that problem. Leave room for a third column. My example above might end up looking like this:

Problem	Likelihood	Consequences	Overall Score
Not many people can come	1	3	
Booze runs out early	2	3	
Uncle Fred gets drunk and does a striptease	2	2	
Someone loses their coat/bag	1	3	
Someone drops red wine on my best rug	2	3	
I over-order on the French bread and am eating stale bread for a week	1	2	
My two sisters have an argument and everyone else is embarrassed	2	2	
People don't like the music	1	3	
My CD player packs up	2	3	
People don't like the food	1	2	
Nobody talks to each other	1	3	
My glasses/crockery/furniture gets broken	3	2	
The neighbours complain of the noise	3	3	
The neighbours complain about the parking	2	2	

Figure 10.1 Assessment of risks

Now you need to multiply the two figures in each column to get an overall score. These would be as below:

Problem	Likelihood	Consequences	Overall Score
Not many people can come	1	3	3
Booze runs out early	2	3	6
Uncle Fred gets drunk and does a striptease	2	2	4
Someone loses their coat/bag	1	3	3
Someone drops red wine on my best rug	2	3	6
I over-order on the French bread and am eating stale bread for a week	1	2	2
My two sisters have an argument and everyone else is embarrassed	2	2	4
People don't like the music	1	3	3
My CD player packs up	2	3	6
People don't like the food	1	2	2
Nobody talks to each other	1	3	3
My glasses/crockery/furniture gets broken	3	2	6
The neighbours complain of the noise	3	3	9
The neighbours complain about the parking	2	2	4

Figure 10.2 Assessment of risks with the overall scoring

Try to eliminate risks

This starts to show which risks are the really serious ones. In this example, the neighbours complaining about the noise is the most serious so you need to think about this one first. What could you do about it? You need to come up with ways of eliminating the risk, or if that can't be done, reducing the likelihood of the risk happening or the consequences of that risk. With the neighbours, if you invited them to the party then they'd be very unlikely to complain of the noise. Perhaps you could go and see if they are planning any weekends away in the next few weeks. Perhaps you could hire the village hall or a room at a pub instead of having the party at home. All of these options could remove the risk once and for all.

Reduce the likelihood

If none of those are going to work, then you'd have to reduce the likelihood of them complaining. Make sure the music is in the room furthest from the neighbours, keep the windows shut and add some heavy fabric to the curtains to deaden the sound.

Reduce the consequences

Finally, how could you lessen the consequences? Perhaps you could phone the local council and police and check what the regulations are. Explain the importance of the event to you and how you've tried everything else and get them on your side, so that if the neighbours do complain it's less likely to have any severe consequences.

Having looked at the risk with the highest score, then you look at the next lot of scores – anything getting a six. That way, if you don't have time to sort out everything, at least you can focus on the biggest issues.

Update your plan

Once you've been through the list, you may well find that you have some additional actions or expenditure. Make sure you update your plan and your budget. Now you have a way forward with an approach which will minimise the chances of you suffering any of the problems you thought of. If you used other people to help identify all the possible problems and have thought of ways to manage those problems, then your chances of success will be very good.

Review the risks regularly

Working out the risks and how to manage them as part of your planning is only part of the story. Just as you need to monitor your action plan and your budget, you need to monitor the list of risks. Things can change and the likelihood and impact of a problem can change too. Suppose you planned to hold your party in the garden. A possible risk to consider would be bad weather. If you were holding the party in June, you might think that the risk is quite low; however, as you get nearer the time of your party you might start to see long-range weather forecasts which predict bad weather. These predictions get more likely to be accurate the closer you are to the date. If the predictions of bad weather continue to appear, it might be time to consider organising some sort of shelter, replacing the barbeque food with a buffet or tidying up the house and clearing away some furniture so that everyone can go indoors if necessary.

However, the reverse can be true and a problem might become less likely as time goes on. When I was training for my triathlon, I did wonder what I'd do if I felt I could not finish the whole race. In order to reduce the likelihood of this happening, I tried doing a 400m swim then sitting in on a one-hour spinning class and then running the distance I'd have to run on the day. Once I'd done that, I reckoned that it was very much less likely that I would not be able to finish the race because I was not fit enough.

The effect of risks might change as well. If I gradually worked down the contents of my freezer so that there was plenty of space, then having too much food left over from the party might not be a problem after all.

New risks

You might also identify new risks which you had not spotted before. This might be either because you had not thought of them or because circumstances change.

The first time we took our alpacas to a livestock show we carefully made a plan which we thought covered everything. We worked out what we'd need to do to prepare the animals, the livestock trailer and the car and what we'd need to take with us. As part of the preparation, we attended a training course on showing alpacas and after that we revised our plans. In particular, we learnt about the diseases which our animals might risk catching and so we added actions to protect them to our list of risks.

Plan for the worst

The key to risks is to keep checking the list and thinking about what might happen. If you plan for all the problems identified then the worst that will happen is that all your contingency plans will not be needed. Sometimes you may not be able to think of a solution to a problem. A very good way to give your brain the best possible chance to think of something is to tell yourself you'll think of a solution in the morning and then sleep on it. It's surprising how well this works. If you still can't think of a solution, ask friends or colleagues if they have any ideas.

The unexpected can still sometimes happen

Of course, you can't always think of everything. In spite of all the careful plans my husband and I had made for showing our alpacas for the first time, just before the show I broke my ankle and that meant a complete review of all our plans. My husband had to take on all the duties of loading and unloading the alpacas as well as taking them into the show ring. Thankfully, our planning efforts paid off in spite of the need for some hasty revisions, including the hire of an electric invalid carriage, and we came away with a first and a third prize. No doubt I'll be remembered amongst other breeders as the one who nearly demolished the show ring with her electric carriage.

Key points

▼ *You can make your own 'good luck'*

▼ *Think of everything that could go wrong*

▼ *Rank all the problems*

▼ *Think of ways to reduce the likelihood of the problem or its impact*

▼ *Keep reviewing and updating this list*

▼ *Accept that you will never think of everything*

CHAPTER ELEVEN

Celebrate Success

If you follow all the suggestions in this book you will achieve your goal. It may be slowly, one step at a time, or much faster if you can multi-task or are good at getting people to help. However you do it, you'll approach the end point, overcoming any problems which may occur by good planning and some creative thought.

Time to enjoy

Enjoy reaching the end

Once you reach the end it's very easy to feel deflated. You may even wonder if it was such a big deal after all. Many of us are too quick to do ourselves down. This is your time to celebrate and revel in your success. Whatever the end point, enjoy it. If it's an event, soak up the atmosphere. If it's achieving a qualification, leave the certificate or letter of confirmation out somewhere and tell yourself how well you've done each time you see it. Give yourself lots of mental pats on the back. Really hold the feeling of success in your mind so that you can recall it whenever you want to. Reward yourself for reaching the target, that way it'll encourage you to have a go at other challenges in the future. You might buy yourself a small treat or have a day off from work doing something you enjoy.

My treats

Whenever I finish a triathlon race now, I always have a post-race massage. I love massages, but it has a benefit too in that it helps prevent injuries and minimises stiffness the day afterwards. The day I published my first book, I went out for a slap-up meal with friends to celebrate. It doesn't matter what you choose to do, but whatever you do, don't just carry on as if it never happened.

Don't focus on the bad points

It can be very easy to only think about what went wrong and the problems you had. You may have some things which you wish could have been better. However, only you know exactly what your end target was and what your definition of success was. Everyone else will probably be impressed that you finished or delivered at all.

Cast your mind back

Think back to the beginning. Can you remember first thinking about the project? Did you ever think you'd get to this point? What have you learnt along the way? Have you done anything for the first time? Make sure you think these things through and, if at all possible, write them down and include a section in your project file on finishing and achievements. Ask the people who helped you what they thought went well and what were the high spots for them and make sure you include those in your list as well.

Think about your successes

Think about all the small successes which have contributed to the project. Think about what went well and make a list. Remember any good times along the course of the project – maybe reaching an intermediate milestone. For my first book, I remember it was great finishing the first draft – actually having a whole book complete. When I finished the second draft and realised that this was a good structure and read really well, that was another high spot.

Pass on your good ideas

Make another list of all the good ideas you had and successful actions which you carried out. Don't hoard the good ideas – pass them on to friends and share what you've learnt. There's nothing like passing on good feelings and success for helping your own success to grow.

When I first started racing triathlons I could not understand how the coaches, who clearly loved the sport, could bear to be coaching rather than competing themselves. However, now that I'm starting to get to the point where I am good enough that I have some secrets of success to pass on, I find that helping other people is actually helping me. I'm starting to think about my actions so that I learn even more from the experience than if I just finished and walked away.

It can be a great boost to morale generally to put some photos or other mementos on display. We often do this naturally for some events like weddings or graduations, but put photos or other souvenirs on display to remind you of your successes. This is a great tool to lift your spirits when you feel down or to encourage you in another venture when problems seem to be driving you off course or the target just seems to be too far away. It can also be used to encourage your friends or family who are thinking of tackling a challenge. It may even be used to persuade people in the future to help with another venture if you show them earlier successes and convey your enthusiasm for success.

I find running the hardest part of my triathlons and so try to enter running races regularly to help me improve. I've never achieved any placing for these races but I've still received a finisher's medal for each race and these hang from the corner of a wall cupboard in the kitchen to remind me, when I am finding my triathlon training hard going, that I have had successes even in my worst discipline.

One of the hardest projects I ever undertook was reconnecting a water supply in the mountains above Sarajevo at the height of the civil war there. When I finished the work, the local council had a large painting made commemorating my visit which had a huge gilded frame. I did wonder where on earth they found the picture frame when there were embargoes and

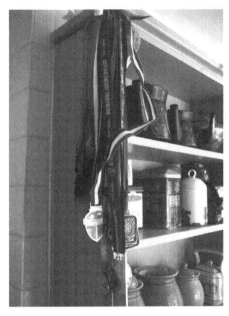

Figure 11.1 Photo of medals

blockades on any goods coming into the country. It was a wonderful gesture but left me with a problem: how on earth would I manage to bring it home as the journey was quite long and I had to stop off in Switzerland for a debriefing with the Red Cross. However, it now hangs on the wall in my office as a reminder that however difficult things seem, it is possible to achieve success. It can boost my morale when I'm feeling rather down and help me find my motivation again. I'm sure you can find your equivalent of that picture when you finish your project.

Figure 11.2 The Bosnian picture in my office

I have put together some presentations of some of my successful projects which I think provide interesting stories and I give talks at local organisations like the WI. I find this has all sorts of benefits. It reminds me of past successes and, in particular, of the feeling when I completed a project. It also encourages other people to have a go and raises money for charity, so this can be a good way to relive your successes and do some more good.

Learn from the process

Of course, there will have been some things which did not go according to plan. Once you have thoroughly celebrated your success, then is the time to think about what could have been better. When I worked with one consultant, after any meeting or activity they would draw a vertical line down the centre of a flip chart page with the letters WWW on one side and EBI on the other. We would first of all think about What Went Well, just as I've suggested to you. Only when we had a really good list would we be allowed to think about 'Even Better If'. It is worth thinking about these things so that you can learn and improve from your experience; what can you learn so that you can do things better next time?

For my first triathlon my list was something like this:

What Went Well	Even Better If
Finished	*Had to walk a little bit of the run*
Wasn't too stiff the next day	*Had to do breaststroke for most of the swim*
Marshals were really encouraging	*Slowest time of everyone for the run*
Remembered to put my helmet on before I touched the bike	*Stopped too long to towel myself dry after the swim*
Got on and off the bike at the right spot	*Took ages to put on cycle top and shorts after swim*

What Went Well	Even Better If
Swam 400m without stopping	*Nearly ran out of the wrong exit*
Managed some lengths swimming crawl	
Overtook some people on the bike ride	
Managed a bit of a sprint for the last 100m	

Figure 11.2 Learning points from my triathlon

From this I knew I had to work on my running and my front crawl. As soon as I could afford it, I also bought myself a special 'tri-suit' which is made of very fast-drying fabric which you can wear for swimming, cycling and running so that I wouldn't lose time drying myself and putting on extra clothing. I always check the beginning and end of both the run and cycle route to make sure I go in the right direction. All these learning points stand me in good stead, even eight years after my first triathlon.

If you prepare a list like this, make sure you put that in your project folder as well.

Of course, some challenges are a one-off. I have no intention of getting married again, whether in the Antarctic or anywhere else. However, I learnt about how to organise holidays and events overseas and I have used some of the things I learnt to help other people planning holidays. I've yet to persuade anyone else to get married on South Georgia, although I have made the suggestion to a few other people!

Ask other people's opinion

It's always worth asking other people for their views on what they think should be done differently in the future. For some projects it may be worth designing a questionnaire – for instance if you are organising an event for the public or for lots of guests. That way you can get ideas for future projects and events, and even offers of help.

Review your action plan

Once you've thought about the good points and what you could improve upon for the future, then it's time to look back at your planning. Look at your action plan. If you have marked on it how long things actually took against what you predicted, where were the biggest differences? Why were things different? Could you improve on your time estimation? Did things overrun? Were there delays you had not expected? Have a look at the budget as well and see whether you estimated accurately for that. Again, if there were variations, why was that? It's useful for some things to check the unit cost. If you had estimated that the catering would cost £200 and in fact it had cost £300, was that because you had underestimated the cost per person or was it because you had more people turn up than you expected? If you understand the reasons for any variations, it will help you develop a more accurate budget in the future.

Review your risks

Finally, think about the list of problems which you put together with the likelihood of them happening. Did any of the problems predicted occur? If so, how did you cope? Did the methods of managing the problems work? If anything else happened which you had not predicted, is that a lesson for the future, or just one of those really unexpected events, like my broken ankle just before our first alpaca show?

Say thank you

When you have learnt all the lessons you can from the project, don't forget everyone else who helped you complete the challenge. A thank you can make a huge difference. Don't forget to say thank you on the day – just a few well-chosen words can make a huge difference to how someone feels about themselves, about you and even about whether they would consider helping again in the future.

Include thank you in your action plan

It may well be worth adding some extra actions to your action plan; for example, buying small gifts, a bottle of wine or some flowers to say thank you to people who have really helped. I had some wonderful help for my wedding. A friend of my husband baked and decorated a wonderful cake for us and I had a beautiful dress made. I visited both people and brought back small gifts for them, although South Georgia is not overwhelmed with souvenirs. I also volunteered to write a letter of recommendation for the dressmaker which would help her in her business and had photos done for each of them – of the cake at our celebratory lunch for one and of my outfit outside the church for the other.

Say it with flowers

One thing I have seen done which is a nice touch is that flowers used to decorate tables or anything else have been given to people who have helped in special ways. If your budget is limited and you have a lot of helpers, then gifts which might seem rather small on their own can be wrapped prettily to make them more special.

Letters or events

After the event, thank you letters can make a huge difference. I know I'm always really pleased when I receive something like that. Another nice way to say thank you is to organise a thank you event for the helpers. This can be a little time later if it's possible that some of them might be rather tired. It does not have to be a dinner or an expensive event; a coffee morning or drinks at the pub can sometimes be appropriate.

Enjoy your milestones

So now if you have learnt all your lessons, celebrated your success and thanked everyone who helped you along the way, you really can consider the project has been completed. I have completed this book and you can be sure I will be celebrating. It's not the end of the project; there are further drafts to prepare, designs to be completed, copy to be edited and publishing to be organised, but a milestone has been reached. I wish you luck and enjoyment with all your milestones, large and small.

Key points

▼ *Celebrate reaching your goal*

▼ *Think about what went well and what could be improved*

▼ *Learn from the process to improve future plans*

▼ *Remember to say thank you to everyone who helped*

About the Author

Jo doesn't know the meaning of the word "can't". If she thinks she can and should, then telling her she can't will only add impetus to her plans. At 14 her teachers told her girls couldn't be engineers. At 24, the youngest age allowed by the Institution of Civil Engineers, she became a chartered engineer. Two years later, when faced with a rotten roof and no experience of carpentry, she rebuilt the front of her house. People describe their building horror stories, she has gone on to renovate and extend three more houses.

When told she couldn't have a job managing manual labour she looked to get that experience overseas. When told she couldn't work overseas as she had no experience, she signed up with a charity "Registered Engineers for Disaster Relief" (REDR) and took a job that no one else would – working with the mujahideen in war torn Afghanistan to renovate the infrastructure in one of the remotest areas. The mujahideen commander told her she couldn't bring the cat she'd rescued out with her, but she did. Her book, Water Under The Bridge recounting her adventures in Afghanistan continues to entertain and inspire readers.

In a second assignment in the mountains of Bosnia she did what the politicians couldn't do – brought Serbs and Muslims together and got agreement to co-operate on restoring water supplies to

Sarajevo. Meanwhile, back at home in her career she was told she was ridiculous to think of being a director. In 2000 she was appointed Director of Operations of North Surrey Water.

Her belief in overcoming obstacles doesn't just stop with her own career. She has been an active member of the Women's Engineering Society and of engineering institutions, encouraging younger people to take up this creative and fascinating career, and mentoring those who have yet to progress in their career. She has maintained her links with REDR and has served on the board of trustees as well as helping fundraising. In 1995 she was awarded the MBE.

Life is not all work however. She is an accomplished cellist and double bass player, having performed in both the Royal Festival Hall and the Albert Hall and is still in demand to play in jazz bands and orchestras. She started racing in triathlons at the age of 47 and has won a number of trophies.

In 2005 besides establishing her own engineering consultancy, she was shortlisted for the newly launched First Women Awards, moved house and got married – in the Antarctic.

So what "can'ts" will Jo disprove this year? Well, in spite of breaking her ankle when working on a water leakage reduction project in Madagascar she has made a return to triathlon and intends to race along the same route as the 2012 Olympics. She will also be expanding another new business she's just started – breeding alpacas. She has taken on 16 acres more land, bought her own stud males and is looking to continue her success at shows this year.

Jo lives in Leighton Buzzard with her husband, two demented Labradors called Rio and Alfie and after the sad loss of the cat she rescued from Afghanistan who reached the grand old age of 19, two further rescue cats from rather closer to home.

Printed in Great Britain
by Amazon.co.uk, Ltd.,
Marston Gate.